In the journey of life there are a handful of people you encounter that define a word. You are about to meet one of those rare individuals in this book. A man that has overcome numerous obstacles, his narrative will inspire you to hope and believe that nothing is too difficult to face when the courageous love of Christ apprehends you. Perseverance in my dictionary is defined simply in two words . . . Canisius Gacura.

~David Pepper, founder, Amazon Outreach

A fascinating read about a man who has overcome many obstacles in his life. The book will inspire you to overcome the obstacles in your life.

~Dr. Dan C. Hammer, Senior Pastor, Sonrise Christian Center, Everett, Washington

Be ready to be challenged, motivated and inspired to go where you have never gone before, to do what you have never done before, and to achieve what you or others thought you would never achieve in your life.

~Pastor Steven Mayanja, Senior Pastor, Seguku Worship Center, Kampala, Uganda

We looked at this small young man and his wheelchair, and at the great mountain that rose up behind the college. But with the eyes of faith and the God who can move mountains, Gacura accepted the challenge. Without complaint and with a joyful heart, he conquered all the mountains set before him. Gacura and his wife Allen and four children have built a great ministry. They have mountain-moving faith to conquer the nation of Rwanda for God.

~Ron and Shirley DeVore, President and Founder, World Outreach Ministries Foundation

This book will inspire you tremendously the way Canisius Gacura's life has inspired me.

~Lovie Phillips, founder, God Loves Kids

UNLIMITED
Conquering
On
My Knees

Canisius Gacura
with
Debbie Maxwell Allen

World Outreach Ministries Foundation
PO Box 23267
Federal, WA 98093-0267
www.womf.org

Printed in the United States of America

First printing 2015

ISBN-13: 978-0-692-56726-5

First Edition
10 9 8 7 6 5 4 3 2 1

Cover Illustration © Copyright 2015 by Lois Rosio Sprague
Cover Design by Scoti Domeij, Blackside Publishing
Editing by Shelly Piazza Worscheck
Author Photograph by Bill Wegner

I dedicate this book to my beautiful wife, Allen,
With all my love and appreciation to God for allowing me to be a
part of your life.

I also dedicate this book to missionaries
Syvelle and Lovie Phillips
and
Ron and Shirley DeVore
Your endless commitment and selflessness
will always be remembered,
and has left fingerprints on my life
that will never be forgotten.

Pastor Gacura endured twelve years without a wheelchair, then returned to crawling during four years of Bible college, plus two more years in Rwanda. This totals at least eighteen years of crawling.

Contents

Foreword

CANISIUS GACURA HAS WRITTEN a book about his incredible life, titled *Unlimited*. It is a fascinating read about a man who has overcome many obstacles in his life. The book will inspire you to overcome the obstacles in your life.

I will never forget the first time I met Pastor Gacura at Seguku Worship Center and Yesu Akwagala Bible College in Uganda. A huge, steep hill leads to the church and school, and the guest house sits on an even steeper hill above. After speaking in the church, I dread climbing up the hill to the guest house. That hill makes me feel like an NFL lineman in the 4th quarter—where are the oxygen tanks when you need them? I always have to stop halfway to catch my breath. It amazed me to discover that Canisius climbed up that hill to school every day on his hands and knees. Not only has he overcome these physical obstacles, but many emotional and spiritual obstacles, as well.

Gacura's life is a testimony to what God can do in a life yielded to Jesus Christ. Pastor Gacura's faith, love and smile are contagious. I love his laugh and his incredible ability to communicate. I have had the privilege of preaching and teaching in his church and staying in his home. He has a beautiful wife and family. He has preached in my church and been in my home. He is a man of faith who trusts God with all his heart.

As you read his story, be aware of what God can do for you like he has for Canisius. I highly recommend my dear brother and friend to you. When I think of him, I am reminded of the words of the Apostle Paul in II Corinthians 4:16-18 (NKJV). "Therefore we do not lose heart. Even though our outward man is perishing, yet our inward man is being renewed day by day. For our light affliction, which is but for a moment, is working for us a far more exceeding and eternal weight of glory, while we do not look at the things which are seen, but at the things which are not seen. For the things which are seen are temporary, but the things which are not seen are eternal." Pastor Gacura has allowed the things that have come against him to work for him and not against him. We can too!

Overcoming polio, abuse, trauma, ridicule, rejection and the like, he tapped into the Unlimited love and power of God. As you read, may you too tap into the Unlimited love and power of God! I love you, Canisius Gacura.

Dr. Dan C. Hammer
Senior Pastor
Sonrise Christian Center
Everett, Washington, USA

Fangs

FIVE MILES. NOT so far. To a boy known as the fastest in the village, five miles was a challenge, not a chore.

I wiped the sweat beading on my forehead and leaped over elephant grass clumped in the small clearings between the jungle trees, the rhythm of birdsong keeping time. The air felt damp and thick as honey with the threat of an impending rainstorm. The thought made my legs churn faster.

I hurdled the wide roots of mango trees. The soldier formation of bamboo flashed past and I felt the sting of the razor sharp grass snap against my bare legs. Shafts of sunlight filtered between the green canopy leaves, painting the jungle with shifting stripes of light and dark.

Uncle Kaytitare warned me to move quickly. The storm clouds increased the need for speed.

More clumps of jungle grass cropped up in the next small clearing. I made a game of leaping from tuft to tuft. Thunder rumbled. The birds and monkeys went quiet for a moment.

Something cold brushed my ankle. I stopped still.

When I looked down, my blood turned to ice. I stared into the gaping mouth of a snake, fangs dripping. That one glance told me—move! The zigzag brown stripes of the snake sent a ball of cold dread to the pit of my stomach.

Puff adder.

The sight of the deadliest snake in the jungle eclipsed my fear of the storm, of being alone, of the soldiers. Every other thought distilled into just one.

Run!

Village

ONE DAY BEFORE...

"Come on, Canisius!" my brother called. "I will race you past the village to the acacia tree."

I looked up at my older brother. "Not now, Joseph. Mbabazi is almost walking. See?" I helped my half-sister take a few steps, then released her right hand. Her chubby grip tightened around my index finger as she found her balance and took another step. I slipped my finger free and squatted a little ways in front of her. "Come on! You can do it!"

Her lips pursed in concentration, and she moved her little foot forward. She wobbled for a moment, before plopping down on her bare backside. With a little wail of frustration, she crawled toward me.

I picked her up and swung her through the air, making her laugh once more. I stepped over a pile of papyrus mats toward Joseph. "Can you imagine not being able to run? Having to crawl everywhere?" I poked Mbabazi's bare belly. "We will try again tomorrow, little sister. Soon you'll be keeping up with me!"

Joseph elbowed my ribs. "Leave her and come race me. There will be plenty of time for children when you're grown up."

I passed the baby to one of my aunts, who paused in weaving a papyrus mat. "I like children. I hope I have a lot of them someday."

Joseph snorted. We kicked off our rubber tire sandals, and with a shout the race began. The acacia tree sat beyond the edge of our little village consisting of the huts of our father, grandparents, aunts and uncles.

I pushed off on the balls of my feet, sending a teasing glance at Joseph. "You will not beat me, you know."

"I am going to try," he puffed. Joseph darted left around my father's hut, hoping for a shortcut.

Sprinting faster, I drove my body down the center path of our village. Though filled with people, my confidence felt high. The chatter of monkeys pushed me forward.

I sped up past my grandmother, Maria, who stirred a pot of cassava in the shade of her mud hut, where I lived. Though the smell tickled my nose, the last thing I wanted was for her sharp tongue to catch me and find something for me to do.

Next, I hurdled the wooden benches in front of Aunt Prisca's hut. She grinned at me from the doorway, her little boy on her hip. Her husband, Uncle Steven Senyange, sat carving a wooden spoon with a red-handled knife.

My feet splashed into a puddle left from yesterday's heavy downpour, my toes squishing in the mud, a constant reminder of the rainy season. From the corner of my eye, I tracked Joseph as he raced behind the huts. Though I had to dodge people, he ended up skirting chickens and goats. Their squawks and bleats sounded funny. I chuckled, pushing off an over-turned bucket.

My stepmother, Christine, waved as she carried a fresh bucket of milk. "Thank you for making the beds this morning," she said as I raced by.

"You are welcome," I panted over my shoulder. "I will fill your woodpile later."

As I passed one family member after another, my smile grew. There were Uncle Kayitare and a cousin, practicing the drum. Here was an aunt tying bundles of dried grass for the roof of her hut. Small children who I cared for and taught to walk. Everyone in my village was a relative, and I was surrounded by love. My eagerness to help others kept me busy every day. Even at the age of seven, I wanted so much to *be* someone. To make people happy. To be generous and full of integrity like my daddy.

Just past the last hut, I glimpsed Joseph shooting like an arrow toward the acacia tree. My confident grin made him frown and pump his legs faster.

Suddenly a dozen or more village children flanked our track—our cousins and siblings come to watch the end of the race. They danced and cheered us on, slapping hands and stomping feet, keeping time with the pounding drums nearby.

I loved the feel of the wind in my face, my callused feet smacking the ground, tilting my head back with abandon. Joy filled me in those moments. The moments when I didn't think about the hardships of life. Just the freedom to move, to run.

I tagged the tree at the same moment as Joseph.

Joseph's face clouded. "It is not fair that I did not beat you. I am four years older."

With a wink, I said, "Who can reach the top of the mango tree first?"

My brother took off for our favorite tree, and I hung back to be sure he had the advantage. Trees were not a problem for me—I often reached the top first. No matter the height or the widely spaced branches, I swung like a monkey from limb to limb, gripping the bark with nimble fingers and toes. Mango trees were my favorite, with their strong limbs and thick leaves. Good for staying hidden.

We climbed high into the top branches. The bark felt rough on the soles of my feet. Joseph sat on a thick branch with one skinny brown arm around the trunk, and I settled into my preferred spot—a branch that split into two, giving me a cradle to rest in.

Beyond the sheltering leaves, the mud huts of our village clustered beneath the trees like resting cattle. The largest grass-roofed hut was the home of the most important person in the village, and it belonged to my father and stepmother. The circular huts sat spaced apart from one other. Men and women moved between the huts and the work areas, repairing tools, pounding grain, and chasing barefoot children. Smoking fire pits beneath steel pots dotted the village view from our treetop perch. Daddy, along with some of my uncles, and a few older boy cousins had traveled out in the bush, caring for my father's cows. Comforting aromas drifted our way—posho, made with maize flour, and beans with vegetables, fried with ghee. My mouth watered, and I wished I had plucked a banana for a snack.

We used only handmade tools and owned few store-bought luxuries. Our homes and furnishings were all handcrafted from the natural resources around us. Daddy was the head of a village consisting of his own family. He ran a little shop in town, and owned a small herd of just over forty cows—barely enough to provide for our village. Wealthy men owned a hundred head or more.

In 1964, at the age of fourteen, due to the conflicts, he fled his homeland of Rwanda, due to conflicts between governing factions. He arrived in central Uganda as civil war was just beginning. I was born in 1978, my mother and father's third child. This was during the last year of the brutal regime of Idi Amin. Amin had held a military coup seven years earlier and deposed the former Prime Minister of Uganda, Milton Obote. After Amin was overthrown in 1979, Obote again regained power, and his tactics were even more violent. Obote's minister of defense, Yoweri Museveni, finally opposed him. From 1981 to 1986 guerrilla warfare raged in Uganda between the Uganda National Liberation Army and the National Resistance Army. The Ugandan soldiers searched for rebels, and frequently raided peaceful villages like ours, believing that the cattle keepers supplied the rebels with food. Estimates of those who died ranged between 100,000 to 500,000 people. Many were raped and tortured by the lawless soldiers. The part of Uganda where we lived was deeply affected, as the rebels hid in the vicinity, and I had already witnessed many of these horrific events. I gazed down from my perch in the tree, thankful that today was a day of peace for our village.

"Canisius!" Grandmother Maria's smoke-roughened voice came from the base of the mango tree. She propped her hands on her bony hips. "Come down. Your cousin brought a message. Your father needs the pesticide. He is at the lake."

This was an order Joseph and I were glad to obey. I was proud of Daddy's herd of cows. They provided highly-valued milk, which was not only a huge part of our culture but brought income to purchase other needed supplies. Ticks constantly irritated the cows, and we relied on the pesticide to keep the insects in check.

Joseph and I slid down the trunk, happy to perform some service like the bigger boys. We ran into Christine's hut. Our step-mother greeted us from the milk room—the most important room in the hut, where she was making yogurt. We entered the room where the pesticide was kept safe, away from the small children. I chose one of the two-liter bottles along with a smaller bottle for measuring the poison. Joseph chose a can that held twenty liters of water. He hefted the large container to rest on his head while I carried the pesticide and the measuring bottle. We set out down the trail toward Wamala Lake.

Soldiers

WITHIN MOMENTS, THE chatter and clatter of the village faded as we moved deeper into the jungle, the rich scent of loamy soil enveloping us in the thick air. The buzz of insects, squawks of parrots, and screech of red colobus monkeys replaced the village noise. From time to time, we heard the stomping of wild pigs, the trumpets of elephants, and even the growl of leopards and tigers in the distance, but those sounds never bothered us. They were just the sounds of home.

At one point, the trail came near what we called the main 'road', a rut-gouged single-lane track. Daddy warned us to stay away from there. Though the road was far easier to travel than the narrow, winding jungle paths, bands of soldiers could appear at any time, and we had witnessed up close how much more dangerous those men were than any wild animals we might encounter.

A low hum sounded from the direction of the rutted road. As the noise grew louder, the jungle sounds fell silent. Joseph and I locked gazes. His brown eyes widened in terror. Without a word, we set down our jugs and leaped for the nearest leafy tree. We scrambled high enough to hide in the canopy.

The hum grew into a rattling, growling sound, that made my grip on the branch tighten. Joseph and I hugged each other, shaking with fear. Between the leaves, a green demon chugged down the road. Soldiers clung to the moving vehicle, which far outsized the lone bicycle that served as transportation for our village. The monster looked as though it could swallow us whole.

Though the truck was foreign, the weapons were frighteningly familiar. The soldiers bristled with guns, and with cloths tied over their faces against the dust of the road, they had a sinister appearance. Wild animals held no worry for us, but a truck? Soldiers? Sheer terror.

Please pass by. Please pass by. I did not know if the ancestors Grandmother Maria worshiped would hear me pray without some kind of offering to bring the message to God, but the prayer for help came instantly to my lips. I dreaded the thought of the soldiers terrorizing our village yet again. God was the supreme being, responsible for all good and bad things on earth. Did he know what was happening to us in that moment?

Joseph and I barely breathed the humid air as the truck lumbered closer to the path leading to the village. *No, no no. Not the village!* I had just celebrated a birthday, and in my seven years I had already seen horrific atrocities. Sometimes they buried people up to their necks and let the birds peck out their eyes. Others they tortured by allowing molten plastic to drip on their skin. These evil men had no conscience and little mercy for women and children.

I remembered the day a band of soldiers stormed into our village. The memory made me grip the tree branch tighter. They took whatever they wanted. They raped the women in turns, and I shuddered, remembering their terrified screams. They beat the men and forced them to carry what they looted from our homes. Some in our village were able to flee, but Maria and I could not. I huddled against the wall inside our hut as they barged in. One of the soldiers grabbed my grandmother's arm and demanded in Swahili that she give him money.

"Leta pesa!" he shouted. "Leta pesa!"

Maria was strong and fierce, always in control. But she only knew the Rwandan language of Kinyarwanda, and these words sounded to her like 'give me buttons'.

She replied in Kinyarwanda, "I do not have buttons." She showed the soldier that she had no buttons on her clothing.

His face became furious and he slapped her hard, shaking her small frame.

Maria cursed him, saying, "How can you dare to disrespect your elders? You slap me when I am the age of your mother. You are a fool!"

Fortunately, the soldier did not understand her words, because these men were bloodthirsty killers. He could have easily taken her life that day.

Another brute rummaged through my father's belongings, taking every piece of his clothing. They slaughtered one of our goats, but fortunately, the cows were safe some distance away in the jungle.

Worst of all, these soldiers, whose occupation should have been protecting the people and their property, seized my father and dragged him away, claiming he was a rebel. Weeks passed, and we believed we would never see him again. What would we do without him?

Hatred grew in my heart for these men who preyed on innocent people. How could a heart become so dark as to make someone do these terrible things? I promised myself I would never be like them.

After the soldiers left with my father, Grandmother Maria made one of her frequent trips to the witch doctor. She provided a hut to keep a witch doctor in the village for emergencies. She consulted with the intimidating man and made some rituals. Afterward, she took ashes from the fire and threw them in the air, in the direction the soldiers had come and gone from our village. She called in a loud voice, "The way these ashes are scattered, may you never come back forever. May you die on your way while you are going, rather than killing and torturing innocent people." After this, she took a big breath, as if she had completed an important task.

Weeks later, Daddy was released.

I was the first person to see him as he stumbled down the path toward our village. His bent form, usually so tall and proud, was barely recognizable. He was stick thin, dirty and haggard. In my shock and excitement, I ran inside the house without even greeting him, so I could tell my grandmother.

She continued her cooking. "Do not tell me lies, Canisius!"

But soon, the whole village cried tears of joy. We never expected to see him alive again.

That night we sat around the smoky fire, and as flames danced and shadowed his gaunt face, he told us his story.

"Do you remember how the soldiers checked my pockets before they took me away?" he asked. "They were looking for Museveni."

We laughed for the first time in a long time, amused that the soldiers thought the famous rebel leader could make himself so small. But the rest of his tale sobered us.

The soldiers tortured my daddy, beating him, threatening him daily with death. He spent days without food and saw many people killed in terrible ways. Of the large group captured along with him, only he and two other men survived. Perhaps God had heard Maria's requests.

At that time, I didn't know much about God. I was taught that we could have access to God through the spirits of our dead ancestors. That was why we needed the witch doctors. They helped us contact our ancestors who could then carry our requests to the supreme God.

A tight grip squeezed my arm, interrupting my memory, and I nearly screamed. Between the leaves of our tree, the truck had slowed even more—near the village trail.

"What now?" Joseph whispered, panic in his eyes.

What can I do? I can run. Running was my life. Everywhere I went, I ran. Almost every race, I won. This would be no different. I would race the soldiers. With my lips at Joseph's ear, I said, "I can run the shortcut to the village. Warn everybody."

Just as I wrapped my shaking legs around the trunk to shimmy down, Joseph grabbed my arm again. "Look!"

The engine groaned, and the truck moved forward, past the village trail. Relief almost made me lose my sweaty grip.

Endless moments passed until the thick foliage hid the retreating truck and the soldiers. Even then, we waited until the sound of the motor faded completely, and the jungle sounds returned. With trembling limbs, we climbed down, landing in a patch of mud. I wondered how long my heart might keep pounding. If only I had some ashes like Maria to toss after the terrible men.

"Oh no!" Joseph cried. "Daddy will be angry that we have taken so long."

I patted his shoulder, my hand still shaking. "Do not worry. Daddy will understand about the soldiers."

And he did. My father, Louis Kinyogote, was a generous man who loved people, always full of smiles and laughter. He worked hard and held high expectations, but he understood about the soldiers.

Carrying the pesticide and our containers, we found Daddy by the shores of the great Wamala Lake, watering the herd with our uncles and cousins. He stood with his hands on his hips, gazing over the water, his muscular calves nearly hidden by the tall papyrus growing at the water's edge. The rippling surface looked so cool and inviting. I wiped beads of sweat from my brow.

Dozens of gray-crowned cranes mingled in the distance. I loved watching these elegant birds. They danced and kissed one another, raising their wings and the furry crowns on their heads.

Daddy turned and spotted Joseph and me, and he and the others helped wave the cows away from the lake edge.

They mooed and lumbered with their bony hips towards the direction he indicated. The cows made a beautiful picture with their colorful hides and long horns. Several were close to giving birth.

"Canisius, bring the pesticide here."

Joseph and I hurried over. Daddy's muscles bulged as he twisted the cap. "Remember my sons, someday you will take over all of this for me. Watch how I dilute the chemical before applying it to the cows. We cannot burn their hide." He showed us how to measure a small amount of the poison into the little bottle, then mix it into the large twenty-liter can Joseph had filled with lake water. We carefully poured the solution over each cow's hide.

I liked watching the ticks scuttle away from the pesticide. I felt more like a man when I helped with grown-up tasks. Daddy smiled with pride as we helped.

Eyeing the lake, I longed to cool off in the waters. I bit my lip and tried to appear as a responsible son should. "Daddy," I said, "Could Joseph and I swim when we are finished? Just a little bit. In the shallow water near the edge?"

His good-natured expression dried up tighter than an old gourd. "Canisius. You know the witch doctor's prophesy."

I shivered at the mention of the mysterious man. We used to dive into the lake all the time without supervision, cooling our hot skin after a day spent helping with the cows. But the witch doctor had declared that one of my father's sons would die by drowning. Ever since, my brothers and I had been banned from one of our favorite activities.

"I can not imagine how I would feel if something were to happen to one of my boys." Daddy softened his answer with a smile and rubbed both our heads. "You are very dear to me."

When he put it that way, I did not mind. At least, not so much. Joseph and I dashed off into the jungle toward the village. Christine's wood still needed stacking.

Besides, I was loved. I was needed. My family depended on me. I was on my way to a bright future—to *be* somebody.

And that felt very good.

Cows

THE NEXT DAY started out promising, with an early dawn race against my friends. I won, as usual. The surly morning clouds gave way to bright sunshine.

I balanced a pot of water on my head, bringing it to Maria for cooking, one of my usual chores. Daddy called out, "Canisius. Go with Uncle Kayitare to look after the cows."

I grinned, happy to be selected for something so important. Uncle Kayitare and I set out along the trail. We stayed on the jungle paths, away from the road. I felt relief to avoid a scene like the day before.

With excited chatter, I dashed ahead, full of excitement. The jungle smelled fresh and clean from the rain the night before, the moisture keeping the dust matted on the path. The cries of jackals and screech of monkeys made me smile.

My belly was full of cool milk. Even without electricity, we managed to keep milk at the proper temperature. The huts were made of mud and cemented with cow dung. In the special milk room, a decorative table was fashioned with mud into a beautiful shape. Every utensil and container for milk, yogurt, butter, or ghee was kept absolutely clean, and used for nothing else. Just one mistake could sour the milk. The milk room stayed nice and cool to preserve this precious commodity. Cows were the major part of our lives, and milk was treasured. When guests came, milk was presented right away.

The five miles passed quickly.

An example of a milk room.

My heart warmed at the thought of greeting my favorite cow, Ntaguranura. Her name meant 'irrepressible'. We named all the cows, depending on their color, character, or behavior. Some cows had horns, either long or short, and some had no horns at all.

Ntaguranura's hide was a rich brown, and I loved her long, curved white horns. She was so well-behaved, and a very good mother. The other cows saw her as a leader, and always allowed her to go first. She obeyed all the caretakers. Her good character enhanced her leadership. I learned a lot from watching her.

Uncle Kayitare and I found the herd grazing in a small clearing. The ripe scent of manure hung in the air. We replaced the young caretakers who had come earlier. They were relieved, as two cows had begun to labor. One of the cows, Abothe, lay on the ground, already starting to deliver. The calf's front legs had emerged, and Uncle knelt down to tear open the sac that clung to its face.

"Do not just stand there, Canisius, go check the other one," he barked.

I ran to the other side of the muddy clearing where Irumba stood. I had seen cows giving birth before, so the sight did not disturb me. Irumba's brown flanks heaved with effort.

"Do not worry, little mama. We will help you," I murmured, stroking her head. I moved to her other end. She was swollen and somewhat bloody, but the baby had not yet made an appearance.

I collected handfuls of dried grasses to scrub the blood and fluids from the hide of the newborn calves in case their mothers were too weary to lick them dry. Over the back of the cow, I watched my uncle expertly guide the calf from Abothe. The mama pushed herself to her feet right away and began to lick the fluids and dirt from her offspring's hide.

Uncle Kayitare grinned and strode over. "She did a good job," he said. His eyes roamed over the second cow. "Irumba seems distressed. Do you see how her flanks heave more than Abothe did?" He checked her hind end, and concern furrowed his brow. "She is not making progress like she should."

My job was to stroke Irumba's head and murmur encouragement while Uncle watched for the calf. After another hour, Irumba sank to the muddy ground with a long, agonized moan. I longed to help speed the process, so she could end her misery. *What must the pain feel like*, I wondered?

"Not good," Uncle Kayitare murmured, one forearm inside the cow's hind end.

"What is it, Uncle?"

"The calf is turned backward. And the contractions are not pushing him forward."

Worry lodged in my stomach. "What can we do?"

"Go and find some strong, thin vines. I will keep hold of the hooves while you go."

I leaped into the trees and quickly found the right kind of vine. My nimble feet dodged trees and roots on my way back. I felt like a hero—so useful.

Uncle Kayitare carefully tied the vine around the calf's hooves, deep in the mysterious depths of the cow. When he slid his arm out, his dark brown skin was shiny with fluid and blood.

"Now, Canisius, you sit by her head and encourage her. I will keep tight the vine, and pull with each contraction to help the baby along."

Laying Irumba's weary head in my lap, I stroked her coarse hair and whispered in her ear. "You can do this, mama. I know this hurts, but you will have a beautiful baby to care for in the end. Think how happy you will be together." But my words poked a tender place in my own heart, for this was not the life I had experienced.

My mother was Daddy's first wife. She also had fled the war in Rwanda, and they met here in Uganda. But my father's business took him away much of the time, and she was left with my fierce grandmother, a woman known for her sharp tongue and control over others. Mama told Daddy how she was treated, and how unhappy she was, but the situation did not change.

In my early years, I was mostly unaware of the conflict between my mother and Maria. But sometimes I found Mama crying, and she would cling to me.

When I was four years old, Mama had enough. She divorced my father, and left without me, my brothers Joseph and Sunday, and my sister, Janet. I always wondered—did she love us enough? Weren't we good enough for her to stay? Maybe it was my fault, that she was sad and tired.

"Canisius!" Uncle Kayitare disturbed my memories. "Push down on her flank. We may be able to save the calf."

With all my might, I leaned my body into Irumba's side. With each contraction, I pushed and Uncle Kayitare pulled. She groaned pitifully, head lolling and eyes rolled back. "Come along! Your baby is almost here," I called.

The moments stretched out. Finally, with a mighty mournful sound from Irumba, the slippery calf slid onto the ground. Uncle gasped with effort as he pulled the baby free. Sweat beaded his skin.

I sat back on my heels, trying to catch my breath. The calf didn't move. "Is the baby dead?" I asked.

Uncle grabbed the dried grass and began rubbing the limp newborn dry. "No, but he is exhausted, just like us," he grinned. "Your job now, Canisius is to get mama on her feet. The baby needs her."

I returned to Irumba's head. "Here mama. You have a beautiful baby. Come see him. You will be so proud." I scratched behind her ears and rubbed her soft nose.

She rolled her eyes to look at me, then closed her lids, sinking her head deeper into the muddy ground.

"Try harder, Canisius," Uncle called.

Both my hands gripped the sides of her head as I pulled. "I know you feel tired. But your baby will soon stand, and he will be looking for milk to make him strong. Come. Please!"

She shifted a bit, trying to obey, but then fell back with a thump. My heart emptied. *Would she survive? Would her baby be left motherless, with no one to comfort him?* These questions were close to my heart ever since Mama left me. New resolve filled my chest.

Tears ran in twin tracks down my face, and my breath hitched. "You must not give up!"

With a mighty groan, Irumba rolled upright and pushed on trembling legs to her feet. I draped my arms around her neck, wishing my own mama had tried harder to remain with me. I felt Uncle's large hand grip my shoulder.

"Good job, Canisius. You have done good work today."

I could only nod, my tears dripping into Irumba's coarse hair, inhaling deeply to calm my breathing. Before long, she turned to care for her baby. At least I had offered comfort to someone else, even though my comforter was no longer here. I looked at the calf with a little bit of jealousy, and let out a long, sad sigh.

Uncle Kayitare glanced at the sun almost directly overhead. "The young ones will not be able to walk the distance back to the village, and we cannot leave them here." He pointed around the clearing. "Animals—or soldiers could easily come during the night."

I thought of the jackals we had heard on the journey here. Those sounds, so familiar and comforting to me, would terrify the baby calves. "We can each carry one of them," I said.

"Canisius, I can carry one, but you are too small to lift the other. You must run home and bring back help so we can keep the cows safe in the village tonight. We do not have much time to make the trip before the sun sets. The mamas will have to go slowly."

I felt a little frightened to travel all that way alone, especially with thoughts of soldiers like the ones Joseph and I had seen the day before. "I will stay with the cows. You will go much faster, Uncle," I said.

"I am sorry, Canisius, but you are too young to remain with the cows. You are the only one to go for help."

The rainy season was upon us and clouds were already gathering for the daily afternoon rainstorm. I did not relish the journey on my own, but I swallowed hard and kept my voice steady. Uncle was counting on me. He said I was the only one to help, and my chest swelled. Perhaps he would tell Daddy how much I had helped today. The thought settled some of my fear. "I will run quickly, Uncle," I promised, heading toward the trail we came from.

"Take the main road," Uncle Kayitare called. "The way is shorter."

A chill passed over me as I remembered the truck full of soldiers with all their menacing guns. Hundreds of people had been killed nearby already. I could not erase the images I had seen, no matter how brave I tried to be. "The jungle is safer. I know some shortcuts. I will go as fast as I can." And before he could argue further I dashed into the trees.

My feet pounded along the trail for the first mile, leaping over roots and rocks, pattering on layers of rotting leaves from seasons past. The shortcut I took should bring me home more quickly. I imagined myself as a hero—a somebody. I would bring help to Uncle Kayitare, and pride would shine in Daddy's eyes. I willed my legs to run even faster.

Snake

THE HUMID AIR stuck to my skin like sap on a tree. Rain was coming, sooner than I thought. I glanced through the dense jungle canopy as I dodged between thick tree trunks. The clouds roiled, the color of a bruise, and they rumbled with thunder. *No matter*, I told myself. My legs were fast. I would reach home first, beating the storm like I won footraces in the village.

To distract myself, I sang a little song in my head, one that my grandmother taught me in the times I missed Mama the most. *Maye hora nguhendahende. Hora nkumare irungu, shira ishavu nshire iringu.* The words gave me comfort. *My dear, stop crying, I plead with you. Let me banish all your loneliness. Do not be sad any longer, so that my loneliness can go away.*

The second mile passed, and thunder sounded again. This time, the distant roll of thunder reverberated closer than before. Scattered drops of rain spit in warning. Now the sky turned ominously dark. As fast as I was, I realized the rain would arrive even faster.

A shiver ran through my scrawny frame. Traveling through the jungle alone was scary enough. But a storm? Rain in east Africa could not be ignored. The fat drops would drill down in torrents, joining together and gushing like a waterfall, determined to wash away everything in their path.

Wishes rarely came true, but I wished with all my heart that the cows had not given birth today. That the weather had been fine. That I had stayed in the village.

I glanced at my surroundings, and my stomach felt hollow. I was still about two and a half miles from my village. Should I have taken a chance with the road?

Dread churned my legs faster.

When tufts of grass popped up along the edges of the trail, I used them to launch myself closer towards home. All at once, I felt something cold touch my ankle, something that was not a drop of rain.

I stopped and looked down. A large snake sat coiled in a tuft of grass. The eyes drew me in and mesmerized me. His mouth stretched wide, and his fangs dripped with venom.

The moment seemed to stretch out until I barely breathed. In the next, I returned to reality. One glance at the zigzag brown stripes on his coiled back funneled all my energy into my legs.

Run!

▲▼▲

There were two things I did not know in those first moments. One I learned seconds later, the other, not for some time to come.

Though I knew this snake was a puff adder, I did not realize the snake had already bitten me. And I did not know the particular dangers of this snake.

The puff adder is one of the most poisonous snakes in the world, mainly because it has the distinction of having both the largest venom sacs of any other snake and the longest fangs. Those two features cause the puff adder to inject a great deal of venom deeply as it attacks. In order to send this poison into its victim, the puff adder unhinges its jaw during the strike. Immediately following the attack, the puff adder yawns in order to reset its jaw.

When I spotted the gaping maw of the snake, cold fear shot down my spine, as I thought the snake was about to strike. I ran with all my might.

Relief surged through my veins as I escaped. But moments later, I felt an itch. I glanced down and saw a few drops of blood on my foot. Had I scratched my foot on a thorn?

When the pain struck, I knew I had not escaped after all. It felt as if a thousand biting ants had converged on my foot and started chewing their way through. I staggered under the intensity, tears pricking my eyes. I was still far from home. Two miles, at least. Yet moving, I realized, would circulate the venom more quickly through my body.

With one deep, shuddering breath after another. I tried mightily to keep from panic. Thoughts raced through my mind. If I waited, would someone come for me? Maybe Uncle Kayitare or Daddy? I quickly pushed that thought away. Everyone in the village knew I was with my uncle. Uncle Kayitare thought I was near home by now. No one knew the exact trail I had taken through the jungle. Staying here meant death.

A sharp crack of thunder shook me from my thoughts, striking terror deep within me. Though I could die waiting for help, I might also die trying to get home. The jungle offered no shelter during the rainy season. No longer did I consider the poison my worst enemy as it worked through my foot. I was forced to do battle with the storm.

Survival meant running. Running fast.

Conquering on My Knees

Needles of rain began to pelt my skin as I fled, favoring my enflamed, throbbing foot. Every few minutes, I looked down. Each glance showed my foot and ankle expanding more and more. It was becoming too much.

An involuntary prayer came to my lips. Please, God, help me. But there was no answer. My heart shriveled in my chest. I was on my own.

The downpour increased as quickly as the pain, both hammering my body. Puddles spread across the ground, creating deepening rivers of mud that threatened to pull my feet out from under me. Within minutes, my left foot and ankle appeared bigger than its normal size. Soon, my rubber tire sandal became too tight. I gritted my teeth and slid it off, leaving it on the trail. The wound burned like a fire consuming me. Blisters began bubbling on the surface—ugly and red. Though the rain came down as strong as a waterfall, at least it cooled my flaming skin.

As the swelling increased, my foot grew heavier, and I soon found I could no longer move quickly. I limped along, dragging my leg behind me like a log for the fire. I felt dizzy, disoriented, weak.

Still, I called out. "Help! Help me!" With the pounding of rainfall, my cries were in vain. I slogged through mud and brand new rivers of water rushing to lower ground. I steadied my balance by clutching slippery trunks with wet fingers. My leg grew so heavy, sometimes I was forced to lift it with my hands.

Somehow, despite the bite, the downpour, and increasing weakness, I made it closer to home. I could not focus on the possibility of losing my leg when the flood could so easily take my life.

Before long, my swollen leg no longer supported my slight weight. I resorted to crawling on both hands and one knee, willing myself to breathe despite the raging pain. Was it only yesterday that I had been teaching Mbabazi to walk?

I reached a deep place where herds of cows passed from time to time, leaving a ditch with no vegetation to keep the soil in place. The water gathered and rushed through here swift and dangerous, yet I had no other choice but to try to cross. I crawled into the flow and my skin chilled with the rising water, which came up past my chest at every dip in the terrain. The torrent tried to run away with me. I grabbed roots and low branches whenever I had the chance, and made my way slowly to the other side of the ditch. My skin felt like a scalding pot and my strength ebbed. I could push myself no farther. I was forced to face a terrible truth. My life would end in the jungle, perhaps a mile and a half from home. Would anyone find me? Would anyone care?

The rain had lessened in the last few minutes, but the reprieve came too late for me. I wrapped my arms around the nearest cedar tree, unwilling to give up completely. I clung to a shred of hope that God might hear my cry for help.

With the last of my strength, I called out, "Daddy! Help me!"

Rescue

I HUDDLED UNDER the tree, gasping through waves of intense burning on my left foot and along my leg. Whenever I could gather a bit of strength, I called out until my voice was hoarse, though I knew it was futile.

Time ticked by, marked by the drip of water from leaf to leaf to leaf. Hazy thoughts swirled in my head, as I drifted in and out of fevered consciousness. Surely this was the end for me. I had so much wanted to be someone. To help others. To make a difference. I was only seven years old and my life was ending.

I turned my head suddenly. Was that a voice?

With every fiber of my body, I listened over the jungle sounds that had returned since the storm passed. Yes! Someone called my name!

"Here!" I gasped, barely able to take a breath as pain engulfed me with the slightest movement. "I am here!"

It seemed to take forever, but finally a face pushed through the bushes nearby. Daddy! He was completely drenched and covered with mud. His eyes widened at the sight of me.

As soon as I saw him, I began to sob. What relief, even through clouds of torment, to feel my father's strong arms around me. I could barely form words between my heaving sobs.

"What happened, Canisius?"

The agony was so great, I could not speak, only moan.

His eyes ran down my leg, and he visibly flinched. He searched his pockets for a cloth, and tied it tightly below my knee.

I sobbed harder.

He lifted me gently into his arms. Tears slid down my cheeks, and I barely had the strength to cry anymore.

"Let us get you home, my son." The bleak expression on his face confirmed what I already knew. There was little hope for my survival.

In the remote area of central Uganda where we lived, the war had taken a toll. Most of the hospitals had closed or were unreachable due to the conflict. The closest hospital was eighty miles away. With just one old bicycle to share for our village transportation, a trip of that distance with a dying boy would be foolhardy at best and deadly at worst, as soldiers continually combed the area for victims.

I remember little of that last mile home as Daddy carried me in his muscular arms. His voice rumbled in his chest like a contented tiger, the vibrations reaching out to me, surrounding me, comforting me. My father's love had always encompassed me. Perhaps these were our last moments together.

The sounds of shouting, wailing, and urgent cries brought me back to consciousness. I did not wonder what was going on—the screaming pain throbbing through my leg reminded me of everything that had happened.

Maria quickly pulled back the sheet on my bed in our hut. Her hand felt ice cold on my forehead and she declared I was burning with fever. Soon, she tried to get me to swallow something bitter, but I became sick with every sip. In my weakness, I could not lift my head on my own.

"Mama!" I called in my delirium.

When Maria saw that the venom had reached farther than my knee, someone tied a rope around my thigh in order to keep the poison contained. The discomfort intensified, as if that were even possible. However, the venom had progressed far since I had been running, and the rope was of no use.

Maria disappeared for a time, and the faces of the rest of my family blurred around me. With my eyes closed in a futile effort to block the pain, I heard their discussion clearly.

"There is little hope."

"If he lasts an hour, I will be surprised, as tiny as he is. A puff adder, his father told me."

"I knew a strong man who was bitten by one. Even reaching the hospital, he died the next day."

"Poor Canisius. I am grieved that Louis will lose a son."

Sometime later, Maria returned. "I have met with the herbalist, who recommends certain items for your injury." She gave me a drink infused with herbs and smeared others on my body and on the wound. She likely had also spoken to the witch doctor in secret.

The herbalist came to see me. "Do not tamper with the wound by cleaning it," he announced. "If you do, it will become much worse. He spoke in a strong voice. "I promise that in a few days, goodness will come of this!"

Through a crack in my lids, I tried to distract myself from the eternal throbbing and nausea by watching Maria.

She stripped the leaves from several plants recommended to her, and then ground them into a paste with a pestle. To this, she added water from the well, along with pinches of dried items she kept stored in the hut.

Maria brought the mixture to my pallet. With the first touch of the medicine on my foot, I screamed. The slightest pressure on any part of my leg—even where it rested on the mat—was excruciating. But spreading the paste felt even worse. My screams kept the rest of the family away, as Maria resolutely applied her homemade concoction to my entire leg. She was a no-nonsense woman and truly believed in the witch doctor and herbalist's instructions.

Some of my relatives came to see me and cringed at the sight of my foot. "Maria," they said, "you must clean the wound. Infection is setting in."

"No!" she cried, her eyes blazing. "The herbalist pronounced that washing would make it worse. Are you trying to be an enemy to my grandson?" People feared Maria's wrath. They took their opinions and left. And so, more and more herbs went in, but the dirt and mud from my crawl through the jungle stayed, festering along with the venom.

At some point, the tourniquet was removed. Oh! The feeling of the blood flowing into the already swollen tissues.

Every hour, I thought I could not have any tears left. But I was wrong.

There was no release from the agony in slumber, for sleep would not come. My stomach convulsed over and over, in my body's feeble attempt to expel the venom. I thrashed in torment and found no position that offered even a small level of comfort.

When dawn's rays lightened the mud walls of our hut, I moaned, my eyes swollen and gritty with lack of sleep. My leg felt as if the snake had bitten me only moments ago. The intense sting and sharp ache had not relented at all.

If anything, I felt worse.

Maria lay sleeping nearby, no doubt exhausted from caring for me since yesterday. I lifted my head, which felt too heavy for my neck, and gazed down at my left leg. I was just a boy, but my leg looked as if it were the size of a man's. Even a light sheet felt like an unbearable weight. I pulled it off.

As daylight grew, I noticed that the skin of my foot and leg darkened. I soon learned that this showed the progress of the venom through my body. The color change reached almost to the top of my knee. Not good.

In addition, the wound from the snake's fangs gaped open, red and raw and oozing.

I looked away. How I longed for my mother. If only she would come. She would understand.

Infection

I COULD HEAR the rhythmic sound of someone chopping wood outside our grass-thatched hut. In my unrelenting pain, I wished that they would come inside and cut off my leg. I doubted it could hurt any worse.

A week had passed. The endless days and sleepless nights ran together, stitched with nausea and misery. Everyone was surprised I had not died, yet I felt death hovering near.

We had no thermometer, and my fever continued to rage. No amount of herbal concoctions or cold cloths made any difference. I retched constantly as my body tried to rid itself of the snake's poison. The resulting dehydration wore on my already weakened body.

I thrashed on the mat. Screaming. Crying. Wailing. Begging. But the torture continued. I could not sleep. Could not rest. Days passed in a haze of blazing heat, sweat, and burning agony.

In the dark of the night, I missed Mama most. Sometimes Maria sat and cried with me, or Aunt Prisca came to hold me for a while. But usually most everyone was fast asleep, and I was alone.

I tried to imagine what Mama looked like. So many years had passed since I last saw her. I dreamed that she came, she put her arms around me, she comforted me. If she had been here, she would have stayed awake all night with me. She would have given me cool water to sip and would understand how I felt.

My world narrowed to my bed, or *urutara* in Maria's hut. No one purchased furniture in those times. Everything was made in the place you lived. Nine holes were dug in the floor. Strong sticks were inserted to support the bed, along with cross-pieces, tied together with rope. After the frame was constructed, a thick layer of dried grass was placed over the top, then a layer of mats, then bed sheets and blankets. But even in this comfortable bed, I writhed.

The skin of my leg continued to darken inch by inch up my thigh, as the venom consumed more and more territory. Large sheets of skin sloughed off from the darkened areas.

And then infection set in.

Whether from the snakebite, or the herbs Maria rubbed into the wound, the already-swollen skin grew an angry red. Streaks, like red lightning, ran higher and higher on my leg. The swelling stretched my skin tighter than a drum and finally pushed past the skin's strength. Great fissures erupted as the skin split open like a ripe melon, offering even more opportunity for infection to take hold.

I didn't think my leg could feel worse. Yet it did.

Daddy paced inside our small hut, wringing his hands, and bemoaning the lack of a vehicle. Maria, in her own fashion, consulted the witch doctor secretly.

But all their efforts were in vain. The wound in my foot and the wounds on my leg widened and grew worse. Besides the hole on the top of my foot where the snake bit me, another hole opened on the sole.

Those who had come to visit me at first, now began to stay away. The sight of my leg made them cringe, and the smell made them gag. The infection gave off an overpowering stench that I could not escape from, no matter how much I longed for a breath of fresh air.

My leg was beginning to rot.

One morning, after yet another restless night, I propped myself up on my elbows and stared with morbid curiosity at the monstrosity that was my leg. The early rays of sunshine reflected on something near my foot. Something white and bloody.

Since I could not reach it, I asked Maria to look for me after she came from the milk room. She peered closely, and her face went pale.

"Oh, Canisius. It is a bone, fallen from your foot."

She washed the bone in a bowl of water and laid it in my hand. It looked like a little stone, except white instead of gray. I rolled it around in my hand, marveling that this object had come from inside me.

That bone was the first of several to escape the great wound beneath my foot. Since the snake bit me on top of my foot, and the bones came from the bottom, before long I was able to see clear through my foot from the top to the bottom.

I wanted my mother so badly. Daddy traveled often to check on his businesses and had just left for another trip.

Within days, a new torture was added. After heaving yet again into a grimy bucket, I glanced at the leg that seemed to belong to someone else—except for the way it felt. Maria took the bucket from me and followed my gaze. She gasped.

Small white things writhed in the open crevices along my leg.

"What is that?" I asked.

"Spirits help us," she whispered. "Maggots."

This new torment, on top of the pain, fever, and nausea, threatened to make me give up entirely. The maggots grew fat, feasting on my rotting flesh. I could feel their movement as they wriggled deeper.

The intense itching and pricking of the grubs became so extreme that I longed to rake my nails into the wide open wounds in an attempt to calm the sensation. At times, I woke from a few moments of slumber to find my fingers red with blood.

Day by day, my body weakened further. Maria told me that whenever Daddy traveled, he feared he would return to find his son dead.

When Daddy arrived home from his trip, about three weeks after my snakebite, he came into the hut to greet me. With one glance at the writhing maggots crawling in and out of my body, he gripped his hair in his hands and cried out in a loud voice. "He is dying. I must help my son." He turned for the door.

"Where are you going?" Maria asked. "I have tried everything the herbalist and the witch doctor said to do!"

The sadness on his face changed to a grim determination. "I know something that may help." He disappeared from the hut.

Daddy returned shortly. He looked as though he had aged ten years in the moments he was gone. When I saw what he held in his arms, a chill went through me.

A two-liter bottle of pesticide.

My eyes grew wide as I realized what he intended to do. He gazed back at me, tears running down his face.

"Canisius." He wiped his eyes with the back of his callused hand. "These maggots will kill you. The infection will kill you. The venom will kill you." His voice broke. "Perhaps the pesticide will give you a chance to live."

Maria's hand flew to cover her mouth. For once, she had nothing to say.

My own voice trembled. "How much water will you use to dilute the pesticide?"

Daddy's face paled. "Diluting the pesticide will not kill these maggots, my son. The only way is to use it at the full strength."

My breath left me.

My eyes could not look away. Daddy's shaking fingers tried three times to unscrew the cap.

"Mama," he said to Maria, though his eyes never left mine. "Hold him down."

"No!" I screamed, reality sinking in. I tried to scramble away.

But Maria's arms were strong, and I had little strength. All I could do was watch as he tipped the bottle over my foot.

Even today, the memory of that experience makes my skin crawl like a never-ending nightmare.

When the first drop of poison touched my inflamed skin, my back arched and I almost leaped from the mat. My screams hurt my own ears. The acid burn was far more intense than I could have imagined.

"There! And there!" Maria grunted, as she nearly laid on top of me. "The maggots are squirming away."

My eyes were closed against the torment, but Maria told me later that the maggots dug deeper, wriggling into my flesh to flee from the blistering liquid. The sensation of their burrowing added to the caustic substance on my tender wounds was too much for me.

My cries went on and on, and my voice became hoarse. My muscles clenched in rigid anguish. I do not know how much time passed, only that I wished I was dead.

Finally, Maria whispered, "They are all dead. I will pick them out."

I was too exhausted to cry anymore, as she used a needle to probe the remnants of my leg. The poison took its toll on the grubs, but what had it done to my flesh?

After yet two more nights of sleepless suffering, Daddy came and stared again at my leg. Some parts of the skin had turned black, and I continued to vomit poison and moan constantly. The expression on his face told me he had lost all hope. He was overwhelmed by what I had to endure. The wound was stinking so badly, I didn't even want to look for myself.

"I do not think his leg can be saved," he murmured.

"I agree," Maria said. "Surviving three weeks has surprised me. But he cannot survive longer."

Daddy rubbed his hands over his face, overcome with emotion. He clamped his eyes shut, then stared at the ceiling for a long moment. Finally, he met her eyes.

"I am going to take Canisius to the hospital."

Maria gasped.

He ignored her. "Perhaps he will live if they can remove his leg."

In my haze of pain, amputation sounded like a good idea. I could not imagine what that would mean for my future.

All I knew was that I was dying.

Maria gripped Daddy's arm with both her gnarled hands. "No. You must not do this. The roads are too dangerous. The journey is too far. You know what happened the last time the soldiers found you. They will assume you are a rebel, and you will be killed. It will all be for nothing." She glanced over at me. "Look at him. He is dying already. A journey like that would take his life quickly. And then you might be killed as well."

Daddy laid his large hands on her wrinkled ones. "Mama. I am going to do something to help. Even if it means to die, let me die on the way to the hospital. He is my son."

Bicycle

THE SUN HAD barely risen, but Daddy prepared for our journey. As I lay gasping and shivering with fever, people whirled around me. Maria tenderly wrapped my leg in a length of cloth, and I wept from the pressure of the fabric against my wounds. Within moments, blood and pus seeped through.

Daddy carried me outside. I blinked in the bright morning light, after my three weeks of confinement in the hut.

My Aunt Prisca waited near the bicycle. Prisca was such a loving, caring person, and had comforted me during the last three weeks. Her white teeth shone against her dark skin, and she seemed to smile all the time. Prisca had volunteered to leave her little boy in the village so she could help carry me to the hospital. If Mama could not be with me, I was glad Aunt Prisca was there.

One of the men held the bicycle as it did not have a kickstand. Forty people in our village shared the single, ancient contraption. It was the shopping cart for market days, the delivery truck for selling milk, the taxi for visits. And now the ambulance.

Christine's hut, with bicycle on the right.

Prisca sat on the seat in the customary way women rode, with both feet hanging off on the same side. Only men rode straddling the bicycle. She clutched the seat with one hand, and held me on her lap with the other while I wrapped my arms around her waist. Exhaustion overwhelmed me already. Though Aunt Prisca tried to hold my legs up, the angle sent more blood to my lower body than laying flat, and I cried even more.

The entire village gathered around as Daddy and Prisca said goodbye. People laid their hands on my head and wished us a safe journey. Their lowered gazes told me that they never expected to see me again. As I memorized all the familiar faces, I did not expect to see them again, either.

One bicycle. One seat. Three bodies. How long would I survive?

Daddy fit his body between the handlebars and the seat that Prisca and I sat upon. Prisca had the difficult job of supporting me while also clinging to the bicycle seat. It didn't help that I cried out with every bump. Daddy's task was even trickier. With the seat occupied, he was forced to stand on the pedals for the entire eighty-mile journey.

Due to the ever-present threat from the soldiers, it was necessary to take the jungle trails, instead of the relatively smoother road. Daddy tried his best to keep the bicycle upright through the twists and turns of the path. He knew many shortcuts, and took those rough trails to shorten the trip. The paths were narrow and the jungle constantly grew inward. Because my legs stuck out from the side of the bicycle, the thorny bushes snagged and scratched my legs over and over again.

I kept my eyes closed, gritting my teeth, and trying not to cry out every time the rough track jostled me. I had run some of these trails countless times over the years, and could visualize all the rocks and ruts and roots that made the bicycle bump and jounce. The pain had been extreme when I laid motionless in bed. How would I endure eighty miles of this torture?

Though it did not rain that day, it had rained recently, and many places on the trail had puddles of standing water. Daddy was not a very good bicycle rider, and he rode through these water-filled holes without slowing down. The stagnant water splashed all over us, as the bicycle had no mudguards. Daddy tried to keep the tires from slipping in the mud, and Aunt Prisca worked to keep us from slipping off the seat. When we reached a hill, sometimes Prisca would get off and balance me on the seat, while Daddy pushed the bicycle up the slope.

Intense chills made me shiver from the fever and constant splashing, despite the humid jungle air. Nausea was a constant companion, only made worse by the erratic movement of the bicycle.

Every so often, we stopped to rest. All of us were exhausted. Daddy's legs felt as weak as a blade of grass. Prisca's arms would start to fall asleep from holding me and trying to protect me from the worst of the bouncing. I wanted to die.

But we continued on. We all had to bear the discomforts. We had nothing to drink for the whole journey, and no food, either, as there was no way to carry supplies on the overloaded bike. I do not know how many times we almost fell off the bicycle. Occasionally, we heard machine gun fire and soldiers shouting, which added the additional burden of fear to our journey.

We pushed on despite the fatigue gripping each of us. Every mile was a battle. I felt so sorry that Daddy had to endure the effort and exhaustion of bringing me to the hospital. But we had no other alternative.

Finally, we reached an area that had less rebel activity, and as a result was not heavily patrolled by the soldiers. The roads were safer to travel, and though there was still some risk, Daddy sighed in relief that we could leave the rough and narrow jungle trails. Due to the rainy season, the road was full of deep ruts and massive potholes, but the task was much easier and we made better time.

Darkness descended, and the journey we had begun at dawn continued. Thankfully, the light of the moon helped Daddy see and avoid the worst parts of the road. I felt myself fading and knew I could not remain alive much longer.

Daddy cried out when he saw the lights of the hospital. We had completed the journey. Noise and activity stirred all around us, people chattering and running back and forth. Soon I was laid on a bed, a real mattress covered with a white sheet. All I wanted to do was rest. In my heart, I believed that once I reached the hospital, the doctors would immediately relieve my discomfort and make me well.

But it was not to be.

Hospital

THE DOCTOR HAD been sleeping at this hour, but when the nurses saw my critical condition, someone ran to wake him. Everyone who entered the room gagged and covered their noses at the stink from my leg. Several had to cover their noses in order to stay in the room. They all worked hard that night to save my life.

The staff gathered around me, examining my leg and discussing different treatments. Everyone exclaimed when they discovered my bite was from a puff adder and that it was three weeks old. The doctor wondered how I could have survived so long without any medical treatment. The wound from the bite was beyond the imagination of the doctors. No one knew of a person, much less a child, who had survived a puff adder bite so long without medical care.

The darkened line of skin that told the venom's progress had reached the middle of my chest. Had it spread just a little further, to my heart, I would have died. The doctors told Daddy that if the journey had taken even two hours more, I would have been dead. He had risked his life on that road to bring me to the hospital.

They began my treatment by cleaning the wound that had become so full of filth. This was excruciating for me. I cried and shouted for someone to help me, but my cries were in vain. Daddy, who I looked to for protection, took the side of the doctors and nurses and held me down so I couldn't thrash while the doctors worked.

I fully expected that the doctors would remove my leg. Though I had dreamed about that possibility in my worst moments, now with medication easing my discomfort I wanted to keep my leg.

With only one leg, how would I move? At what job could I work? How could I be somebody? I had never met a person who was crippled, and worry ate away inside me, much like the maggots. The doctors told me that it was important to remove all the dead tissue if they were to have any chance of saving my leg.

They gave me injections and tablets to swallow, both of which I had never seen before. Day after day the uncomfortable treatments continued. I cried out for my grandmother, but of course, my voice could not reach eighty miles. I felt they were doing more harm to me than good. I began to look at all the hospital workers, and even Daddy, as the enemy for the pain they were causing me to feel.

Daddy had to leave many times to take care of business and family responsibilities. Aunt Prisca stayed with me the whole time. She worked very hard and comforted me greatly. I know she sacrificed much in order to be there with me, including not being able to care for her little son.

At last, after days of medicine, cleansing of my wound, cutting out the rotten flesh, stitching my leg together, and applying plaster, the doctors made the decision. I would keep my leg.

Oh, what happiness! I made up my mind to cheerfully endure everything that must be done to bring healing, and to be patient as the days turned into weeks. I felt like I had been in bed forever.

I missed home. I missed the activity of the village. The smells of my favorite foods cooking. The cool of the milk room.

After a month, I wanted to try walking. The doctors wished I could wait a little longer, but I felt like a prisoner at the hospital. Seeing other kids running and playing outside the window made me long to be with them. Because of the bones I had lost in my foot, my toes would not reach the ground when I walked, and running was not possible. Yet my sadness lifted when I could at least walk a little bit.

My left foot looked nothing like my right foot. The toes were deformed, and the shape bothered me. I tried to focus on the fact that a strange-looking foot was far better than having my leg amputated.

My leg began to heal slowly. Someone was always with me when I walked—I could not be left on my own, as the wound in my foot remained open on the top and the bottom, and could get infected again. The doctors and nurses were so kind to me and loved me greatly, and I tried to obey their instructions.

All in all, I spent over two months in the hospital. One day, the doctor sat down by my bed with a serious expression. "Canisius, you have been a very brave boy. We will be sad to see you leave us. But I must tell you something. Although we were able to save your leg, your foot suffered much damage. I am sorry to say that you may have difficulty trying to do all the things you did before."

I laid my hand on his arm. "Thank you, doctor, for caring for me. Without all of you, I would have died. I will do my best and be grateful."

But despite my brave words, when the doctor left, I turned my face to the wall and cried bitter tears.

It was time to return home and face my new life.

Daddy, Aunt Prisca and I returned home again on the old bicycle. Aunt Prisca's husband, Steven, had borrowed another bicycle and came to meet us, so now we had two riders.

We started very early in the morning. This trip was much less painful than the one to the hospital, and I couldn't wait to arrive home. Every time we stopped for a break, in my heart I said, *Why are you stopping again? We will get home late after everyone is asleep.* I longed to embrace every family member and see the familiar faces I had not seen in months. I had never been away from home so long before. My heart chanted, *Hurry, hurry, hurry.*

Finally, we arrived in the village after the sun went down. Everyone raced to see me. They greeted me with so much joy, as they had lost all hope of seeing me again.

"We want to see your foot," they said.

Since it was dark, no one could see very well, but my leg looked so different from the months before, even though the wound on my foot had not closed.

Most of the family gathered around us, listening to our stories, until midnight. They were amazed at what had happened and considered my recovery a miracle. So many were amazed at how important doctors were in helping me to heal, as we had depended on witch doctors for so long.

For me, being among my brothers, sisters, grandmother, grandfather, aunts, uncles, along with nearby friends and neighbors brought so much joy. Though I could only walk a short distance, and not even into the bush, I felt content to be at home. In the following days, I told my stories again and again. Traveling so far and being treated in a real hospital seemed exotic to my friends and siblings.

Some weeks later, our village learned more good news. On January 26th, 1986, the Ugandan government was overthrown by Museveni, the rebel leader. Finally, the violence and oppression would cease. People danced and sang and celebrated the liberation day.

However, my happy weeks at home were short-lived. Walking in the bush was impossible due to the open wound on my foot. Daddy decided that since my foot wound refused to close on its own, I must stay in the nearby town of Maddu, where nurses could follow my progress at Maddu Health Centre. The town of Maddu sat about ten miles away, near the western edge of Lake Wamala, where Daddy owned a small house and store.

Though I was sad to leave my family for another long period, that February I rode the bicycle again with excitement this time. My anticipation came from the opportunity to finally attend school. The distance from our village made the idea of school impossible for all the children in our family. Pride filled my chest at the thought that I would be the first of our village children to go to school—even before Joseph and Janet, who were older.

Being somebody finally seemed within my reach.

Mama

THE BRIGHT COLORED parrots jumped from branch to branch, squawking loudly, and I wanted to join their song. Seven months after the snake bit me, life was beginning to improve. I didn't mind the frequent rain and mud—I was thankful I could walk and go to Maddu Catholic Primary School.

My friends easily ran ahead of me with my awkward gait, but I had to grow accustomed to no longer winning races. I focused on gratitude for being able to join my friends at all, instead of complaining of my lost freedom. I walked on my left heel, as my toes would not reach the ground due to the missing bones. The wound in my foot had not completely closed, and rubber tire sandals protected my still-tender foot from the thorns and rocks on the path. Though I longed to

climb trees and kick a ball with abandon, I realized the need
to be very careful to avoid injuring my healing body.

A medical dispensary had been established in the
town of Maddu, though the long war had depleted their
supplies of equipment and medicine. The venom had done a
good job of poisoning my leg. Long months dragged by
before the wound finally closed, and the healing skin on my
leg and foot still required regular treatments.

Daddy's small house in town had an attached shop to
sell household goods. Unlike the mud huts of our village, this
house was modern, made of bricks, with iron sheets for the
roof. He paid Anna-Maria, one of his employees, to care for
me there since his businesses often kept him away. Anna-
Maria was kind and attentive, though I missed my family and
the activities of the village.

Anna-Maria was a staunch Catholic, and such a
committed lady to her church. I remember watching her pray
through her rosary beads several times a day. The clicking of
the beads was a comforting sound.

Anna-Maria took me to the Catholic church every
Sunday. I had never attended a church of any kind and was
fascinated by the music, the repetition, and the way things
were done. I thought the priests must be the holiest people on
the planet.

"Maybe I will be a priest someday." I spoke to God, but I did not think he really heard me. I wanted God to hear me, but I didn't know how to reach him. I wasn't holy, like the priest. I didn't have special rosary beads like Anna-Maria. I was a 'nobody' to God.

One day after school in May, I practiced kicking around a ball made of rags in front of the house with my good foot. A man came along, followed by a woman and a young girl. The man pointed to Daddy's house and said, "This is the place." Then he walked away.

The woman stood there, fingering the edge of her headscarf. After a long moment, she called out. "Do you know me?"

I gazed at her, pursing my lips. "No," I said.

The woman edged closer. Her eyes seemed to read me like my teachers read books, the way they scanned me from top to bottom. When she took in my deformed foot, her hand clapped over her mouth, and she started to cry.

She knelt and threw her arms around me, sobbing.

My body stiffened, unsure why this woman acted this way.

"I am your mother, Canisius! I am so sorry that you do not know me. I am your mother."

Mama! My heart filled with joy to see her. My tears would not hold back. She wept when she learned about all I had gone through with the snakebite, and we dried each other's tears.

And she brought a surprise.

I was four when Mama left, and I did not know she was expecting another child. My little sister Catrine was adorable, with bright brown eyes, and a smile that filled a hole in my heart. She was nearly three years old already.

What fun to play with a little sister! Catrine brought such joy into my life, and I did not feel so lonely for family.

"Mama," I said that night, "Why were you gone so long? Why did you stay away?"

"Oh, Canisius," she said, brushing my forehead with her soft hand. "The war was a terrible thing. Obote's soldiers took the cattle from those of us who were cattle keepers. We had no milk; nothing to eat. Bullets seemed to fly in every direction. To survive, we were forced to flee to Tanzania. Have you learned in school that Tanzania is our neighbor to the south—on the other side of Lake Victoria? They have been peaceful in recent years."

I nodded, remembering the map on the wall at school.

Though I felt I was a big boy now, Mama gathered me on her lap and rubbed my arms. "The journey was treacherous. Many died on the way, shot by soldiers. Others developed sleeping sickness and did not survive, or perished from lack of food."

I leaned back, watching the faraway look in her eyes. "I will not tell you more. Despite many terrible moments, Catrine and I survived, and we came as soon as we could. My heart is glad to come and see you growing so strong. I am proud of you, my son." She hugged me tightly, tears in her eyes. "Now, go and play with your sister."

Only years later, did I learn more of what had happened during the war. The evidence has remained—thousands upon thousands of skulls silently testifying of man's depraved hatred and quest for revenge. A testament to the brutality of Milton Obote.

We enjoyed being together, but soon the reality of life intruded. Two days later, Mama told me it was time for her and Catrine to go to the village and see the rest of the family. I longed to go with them but had to remain for my treatments and school.

That farewell tore at my heart. To have Mama back for only two days was not enough. And Catrine. Her jolly spirit made me laugh, and her smile was the brightest.

The three of us parted in tears, Catrine leaning towards me from Mama's arms as they walked down the road. I watched them go until the jungle swallowed them.

In the weeks to come, I would gaze in that direction whenever I missed them.

Spots

OTHER THAN MY treatments, life was pleasant because school continued. I had looked forward to attending school for years before the snakebite and knew the distance of our village from the school would make education impossible. How strange that the snakebite gave me the opportunity to learn.

Walking to school with my books and notebook filled me with pride. Though I did not yet have a school uniform, the clean, white pages of my books made me so happy. I made sure to keep my school things and clothes in perfect condition. Even after only a few months, I genuinely loved learning the sounds each letter made and longed to begin reading soon.

One June day, when school finished, I followed my friends on the path toward the house where I lived. I waved goodbye to my schoolmates at the door, and slipped inside, enjoying the cooler air away from the beating sun.

Anna-Maria greeted me in the main room. She was not alone. A couple with a fussing baby sat at the table. Gafirifiri and Nyirangazari introduced themselves as relatives of my daddy.

"Kisembo is very sick," Anna-Maria explained, nodding at the restless infant. "They have come from their village to bring him to the dispensary."

My heart softened to hear the baby cry. His hoarse wails and lethargic limbs reminded me of my sickness from the snakebite. Both parents looked exhausted from their journey, and perhaps the baby's sleepless nights.

Anna-Maria rose to begin preparing the evening meal. Looking at my schoolbooks, I made a decision. My homework could wait.

"Let me hold him for a while," I offered, limping closer. "I miss the babies in my village. Go lie down for a while. You will have a long night ahead before the dispensary opens tomorrow."

The couple quickly agreed. They retired to a bedroom, and I cuddled one-year-old Kisembo. I loved his round, chubby face, covered with little freckles. He fussed and flailed his fat arms and legs. Singing songs and rocking seemed to calm him somewhat, and once in a while, I could coax a smile. When that happened, it felt like the sun had just risen over the hills. Sometimes he found a little energy to play, but he tired soon after. I paused now and then to wipe his runny nose and the tears from his swollen pink eyelids. He coughed piteously and refused the spoonfuls of milk I gave him to drink.

When I held him to my shoulder and laid my cheek next to his, I realized his fever was very high. I recalled how hot I felt during my own fever. I laid him down and unwrapped the cloth around him, frowning at the sight of more tiny freckles covering his brown skin. Was he born with so many freckles, I wondered?

Kisembo and I spent hours together while his parents rested. I was grateful to help someone, to do something important. Remembering the lonely nights when I longed for my mother's comfort kept me on my aching feet, whispering soft words to the agitated baby.

The next morning, Gafirifiri and Nyirangazari took the baby to Maddu Health Centre, and I made my way to school, bleary-eyed but joyful. I looked forward to caring for Kisembo again after school. Being useful felt wonderful.

However, upon my return, I found Anna-Maria and Kisembo's parents wailing in the yard, holding the baby. Poor baby Kisembo had died that day. He was diagnosed with measles, and there was nothing to be done. What I had thought were freckles were the spots of disease.

Tears slid down my cheeks, and my arms felt empty. How could this happen? The baby's parents were weighed down with grief. If I felt such sorrow after only one night with their little baby, how much more was their suffering? Why did God allow so much pain and misery in this world? These were difficult questions for a boy about to turn eight years old. This was the first time I had seen a dead body up close, and fear settled in my belly. Every time I thought about not seeing Kisembo again, I cried.

Gafirifiri and Nyirangazari returned to their village empty-handed, after journeying to the dispensary with such hope. The rest of the week, I felt sad and despondent.

When I felt the tears come, I limped behind the house so no one could see me. I spent time thinking about Kisembo's beautiful face, and his sunny smiles. The thought of no longer playing with him broke my heart.

When the new week began, I felt no better. Usually I leaped from my bed long before the start of school, but now I lingered, wondering why I was so tired. My eyes felt itchy, but Anna-Maria told me I just needed more sleep. I pushed on, unwilling to miss even one day of school. Ugandan children usually begin school at age three or four, and catching up to my peers had become my mission.

By the next morning, I knew I would not attend school that day. The familiar feeling of chills and sweats woke me in the early hours.

I must have a cold, I thought to myself. There was no purpose in awakening Anna-Maria, as nothing could be done until dawn. I tossed and turned, coughed and sniffled, until the square window turned from black to charcoal.

Before long, Anna-Maria appeared in the doorway. "Canisius. Why do you lay in bed again? Time to get ready for school."

I lifted my aching head to look at her. "I am sick, Anna-Maria."

Her stern expression changed from serious to shock. "No! It cannot be!" she twisted the edge of her blue blouse in her fingers.

I looked down, confused. But the morning light told the story. Freckles dotted my dark skin. Freckles just like those that took the life of baby Kisembo. My head fell back on the mat.

Measles. Why me? I wondered. Have I not endured enough already?

Anna-Maria sent a messenger to the village to inform Daddy, and she carried my shivering form to the dispensary. The nurses were hesitant to bring another contagious patient into their building.

"Besides," they said, "there is nothing we can do for him. We have no medicines. He needs a hospital, with doctors and supplies. You must travel to Bukalagi."

Thoughts of my hospital visit just last year dropped a ball of dread in my belly. I had only been out of the hospital for five months. We returned to the house and Anna-Maria laid cool cloths on my forehead.

Daddy arrived early the next day with Mama, as she was still visiting our family in the village.

Oh, what a comfort she was! This was what I had missed during the days after the snakebite. Someone to care for me and identify with my pain as only a mother can. She bathed my fevered body and held me as I coughed. My armpits felt so sore—the clinic nurse said my lymph nodes were very swollen. The rash felt itchy and uncomfortable, but the fever completely sapped my strength. I felt my will to live draining away once again. I thought about baby Kisembo. Would I die, too?

Daddy agreed that my condition was critical, and the hospital was my only option. From Maddu, the trip was less than one hundred miles, however, we were not in the village where we could use the bicycle. He went from house to house, looking for a vehicle that we might borrow, but nothing was available. Finally, he returned.

"I found a farmer with a tractor who is going to bring sugarcane from a plantation near the hospital. He is willing to let us ride with him. We must leave immediately."

After my restless night, I felt feverish and uncomfortable. I wanted to stay in my bed. Mama bundled me in blankets while Anna-Maria prepared food for the journey. Soon the rumble of the tractor sounded outside, and Daddy swooped me up and carried me into the balmy morning air.

The red tractor loomed over us, growling louder than a thunderstorm. Though my hospital stay had helped me become more accustomed to vehicles, I had never ridden in one before. I hid my face in Daddy's chest.

"My son, it will be all right," Daddy murmured. "The tractor will not hurt you. We must bring you to the hospital with all speed. Trust me, Canisius."

And I did. I knew he loved me and wanted the best for me.

The tractor pulled an empty wagon that would eventually be loaded with sugarcane. The wagon looked in terrible shape, and the paint had peeled so badly that the color was impossible to determine. Daddy paid the farmer, then made a place for he and Mama to sit in the rusted wagon bed. Mama held me in her comforting arms. As we pulled away, rain began to fall. A worried-looking Anna-Maria waved goodbye. Despite my chills, I was grateful for the presence of both my parents.

The journey seemed long—perhaps as long as the bicycle trip last year. At times, I thought the bicycle might have traveled faster than the tractor. The vehicle and trailer had no springs, so whenever we hit a major bump, we flew into the air and came down hard.

The rain did not stop, but instead, grew more intense, which increased my shivering as we could not stay dry. The farmer tried to avoid the largest holes. Water filled each one, and when the great tires went into them, we were splashed again and again.

When we paused briefly for the farmer to stretch his legs, I questioned Daddy. "Why me? Why do I always have these things happen? Perhaps God is punishing me."

He looked down at his work-roughened hands. "I do not know, my son. I hope there can be a reason you will find someday." I saw that my words bothered Daddy a great deal.

Though I asked him these questions, I really wanted to ask God. If he was so powerful, why did he allow such things like cruelty and suffering and the senseless death of little babies? People like the violent soldiers surely deserved tragedies instead. That would seem just.

The rain-filled journey took the entire day before we reached the hospital. Again, the doctors told Daddy that I was close to dying. They were not sure I would survive.

Days blurred into weeks and the skilled doctors and nurses who had cared for me after the snakebite worked tirelessly to save my life again, with strange-smelling medications and injections. I was so grateful for their efforts.

Three long weeks passed until I was strong enough to return home in the middle of July. This time, we traveled by bus—a great novelty. After overcoming my fear of the tractor, the bus seemed tame by comparison. The bus arrived at the hospital three times each week, and I vibrated with excitement as we waited for it to arrive.

Though the bus was old and rusted, it seemed a great adventure for me. As it hissed to a stop, I raced toward the door, ready to jump aboard. But then I stopped myself, remembering that good behavior was an important reflection on my father's reputation.

We settled in our seats, and I begged Daddy and Mama to let me sit beside the window. I bounced on the springy seat, unable to wait for the driver to begin the journey.

With my nose pressed against the smudged glass, my eyes widened to take in all the sights. The trees seemed to run beside the bus. Never had I gone so fast before—not even running at my top speed! That ride was a great experience. We arrived back in Maddu late in the evening, and I departed the bus with sadness that our journey had come to an end.

Soon I was able to rejoin my classmates. After missing so much school, I felt sad that my friends were learning to read a little bit while I remained at my former level. I determined to work hard and learn to read before the end of the school year.

Besides studying, playing with friends was my favorite way to spend the hours. The month of August passed and September began. Though I had only attended school a total of four months, I felt confident that my education would help me to become someone important.

I was on my way.

Polio

ONE MORNING IN September, I awakened as the parrots were just starting to call to one another in the trees. The morning breeze rustled the banana tree fronds.

Time to get up, I thought. But my body felt an unusual heaviness. Perhaps I tired myself too much yesterday.

Anna-Maria scolded me for picking at my breakfast, but I assured her I was fine and made the walk to school. Once there I sat straight, listening to the teacher explain something about Ugandan history, but my brain felt fuzzy like it was wrapped in a heavy blanket. I shivered and blinked burning eyes.

"Canisius?" my teacher called. "Why do you hang your head?"

I rubbed my eyes and straightened to look at her, scrunching my face against the dizziness I felt. "I do not know. I feel tired."

She stepped between the benches, her long dress rustling around her ankles. "Your eyes are red," she said, brushing her hand over my forehead, "and your skin is very hot. You must go home until you feel better."

My lower lip must have stuck out far enough for a bird to perch on as I walked home. Sick again! The measles were done, so surely this was a mild illness. I kicked a stone out of my way. I felt sick to death of sickness.

The new school term had begun two weeks before, and I felt annoyed to miss anything that would delay my learning to read.

Anna-Maria fussed over me and put me to bed, declaring that the fever was very high. "If you don't feel better soon, we will go to the dispensary."

When I awoke that afternoon, my sweaty limbs told me right away the fever had broken. What joy! The sounds of my friends returning from school sent me racing to present my cool forehead to Anna-Maria, who reluctantly agreed that I might go and play.

"Be careful, Canisius. Don't run wild, since you felt sick this morning," she called as I limped from the yard.

Not only was I an active boy, I was stubborn besides. Soon I was playing, running, jumping, and wrestling. We boys enjoyed play-fighting, to see if we could best our opponent, or make him run away. My close friend, Denis, and I joined in a game of football, and we took turns sending the ball to the goal. At one point, I cut in front of him and tripped on his foot. Laughing, he helped me up and I brushed myself off. Of course, I could not run as fast as I used to, but oh how wonderful it felt to be among friends.

But just about the time when mothers began to call their children for supper, I started to feel weak and dizzy again.

I waved to my friends. "I will see you tomorrow."

On the way home, I knew that the fever had returned—and even more intense than this morning. This made me discouraged, as I thought I might miss another day of school.

But even before I reached home, my joints began to throb with intense pain, and by the time I collapsed into Anna-Maria's arms, I had no more thoughts of school or playing or anything else.

My condition grew worse and worse. I felt as if someone took a scorching knife to scratch my bones. Toes, ankles, knees, backbone—every joint in my body felt on fire, with the exception of my hands.

Anna-Maria laid me in bed, but I could not find a comfortable position. I cried and screamed. I rolled on the bed, whimpering. I sat, I knelt, I laid flat—but the throbbing was too much.

"You must have wrestled with your friends and hurt yourself badly. Perhaps you have pulled a muscle or broken a bone—even your back!" She twisted her hands together, and her lips moved. I knew she was praying, to the Catholic God, but what was the use?

"I did not fall down or hurt myself," I gasped.

"I do not believe you."

Anna Maria called all my friends to come. "What happened to Canisius? Who has hurt him?"

My friends shrugged their shoulders. "He seemed fine when we played today." I could see from the expressions on their faces that they felt sorry for me as I lay moaning on my bed.

Denis stepped forward. "We were playing football, and Canisius fell down."

This made me smile despite the sharp ache. "Yes, Denis, you caused me to fall down."

But both of us knew that my fall was a simple thing, and was not enough to cause the level of discomfort and fever I had.

After they left, I began to feel sick to my stomach. I tried to stand to make my way to the latrine, but my legs collapsed beneath me. Just three hours had passed since the fever returned.

I never walked again.

The whole night alternated between crying and vomiting, with no end in sight. It felt like I never rested at all. Beyond all that, dread filled me at the thought of yet another trip to the hospital. For this sickness felt like death even more than the measles.

Anna-Maria didn't know what to do, but she brought me to the dispensary the next morning. It was a Friday—market day, but so early the sun was not up yet. Anna-Maria carried me on her back. She stopped and spoke with someone. In the haze of my fever, I did not even recognize who it was. Anna-Maria asked them to carry a message to my village that I was very sick. She worried a great deal, as she knew Daddy had traveled far away to explore a new location to move the family. The grass in our area had become over-grazed with all the cattle keepers, and milk production had dropped. He felt a new area for grazing could solve the problem, and increase our income.

At the dispensary, the nurse said my fever was very high. She remembered me from three months before, when I had come in with the measles. When Anna-Maria told her about my joints, her lips pinched together, and she left to find another staff member.

They conferred with one another, scratching their heads at my condition. I received some medicine for the fever, and they advised me to return the next day.

On Saturday morning, after another sleepless night, my condition worsened. I could not even sit on my own.

I cried in my mind, God, are you real? Are you loving? Are you caring? Does my life even matter to you?

My stepmom Christine, and Aunt Prisca's husband Steven arrived midday from my village. Seeing familiar faces was comforting, but I could not even express myself, such was my critical condition.

I did understand from listening to their conversation that Daddy's trip took him 450 miles away, to a region that had no telephone. No one knew when he would return.

The fear on everyone's face worried me. After several more days of agony and daily trips to the dispensary, the pronouncement was made.

Polio.

Some people develop polio and get a little bit sick. For others, the disease goes to their lungs and they have difficulty breathing. The most severe form of polio attacks various joints, usually causing paralysis. My case was this last kind—and more severe than most. The clinic workers had tears in their eyes when they told us that they had no resources to help us.

My family transported me to another clinic. There, the nurse shook her head. "This sickness cannot be helped here. I am sorry you came so far. We can transfer him to a hospital. Perhaps they can help."

My family discussed the decision at length. Their words filtered in and out of my feverish brain.

"Don't you see? Even medical doctors cannot help him. In fact, the doctors might make him worse. Death is common from this form of polio."

"They said we can try to make him comfortable, but why not take him to a traditional healer?"

"Yes, their power can be greater than those who learn medicine in school. A traditional healer is the only solution." Traditional healers were different from witch doctors, in that they did not use witchcraft, but folk medicine.

After we arrived back at the house, neighbors and friends began gathering, each with their own opinion. Every person believed that one traditional healer or another was the strongest. Everyone had a story of some terrible illness that had been cured by the healer they promoted. The list of possibilities grew longer. Christine felt strongly that I needed to see a medical doctor, but the others were louder and more convincing. Finally, they chose a traditional healer by the name of Mulego.

My skin crawled at the memory of Maria's witch doctors with their herbs, fetishes, and rituals, even though I knew traditional healers were not the same. I wished Mama was there. I wished Daddy was there. I wished there was a God in heaven who cared about my suffering.

But there was no one.

Treatment

MOST PEOPLE SPEND time wishing they were rich. That they have enough money for anything they need. Although we were not considered wealthy, my father's cows, instead of being a blessing, had become a lure for greediness.

I had no thoughts of this yet as I found myself once again, tightly held by Christine on that old village bicycle while Uncle Steven pedaled unending miles to the prominent traditional healer that had been recommended.

Another uncomfortable ride. Another moment near death. I felt too weak to cry, and though Christine's arms around me were gentle, they caused my flaming joints to scream at every movement.

How many joints does a body contain? I wondered. There must be hundreds, for me to hurt in so many places. Each bump in the road jostled my aching spine.

The dispensary workers had explained that this form of polio destroys both the joints and something called 'nerves', the source of my never-ending pain. I wished I would pass out so that I did not have to endure the trip.

Uncle Steven turned onto a narrow jungle trail. In my hazy memory, we passed a few other huts, asking at one for directions to the healer's home. At long last, we stopped in a clearing containing a single hut.

Two young men, the traditional healer's helpers, came out to greet us. They invited us to enter. Christine picked me up once again, and my head sagged against her shoulder. My eyes took a few moments to adjust to the dim interior.

An old man, perhaps in his sixties, sat in the center of a cow hide spread on the floor for a carpet. He was light-skinned and wore a cloth around his waist instead of trousers. Lines crossed his face, like the roads on the map at school, and his expression looked fierce. My shivering increased, and not only because of the fever.

He indicated two wooden stools covered in cow hide for Christine and Uncle Steven to sit on.

"Welcome." His voice sounded like rocks grinding together. "Would you have some milk?"

Uncle Steven and Christine both nodded, and milk was brought in. I took a small sip, then pushed the milk away, afraid that I would expel what I drank.

Uncle Steven introduced himself. "I am Steven and we live in a village outside Maddu. My nephew here is the son of Louis Kinyogote, a cattle keeper and merchant in our area. His son, Canisius, is afflicted with polio, which gives him great pain and takes the strength of his joints. The doctors say they can not help him. He can no longer walk. Is there anything you can do?"

Though fearful of this man, I watched his face closely as Uncle Steven spoke. The healer's expression had changed from wariness to wiliness as he listened to the story of my illness. I believed that once the healer heard about Daddy's cows, he knew that before him was the son of a desperate man with something to trade.

Mulego smiled, but it was different from Daddy's eye-twinkling grin. "Of course, Steven," he said, spreading muscular arms wide. "I am going to help your nephew immediately." He snapped his fingers as if to show how quickly he would treat me.

I couldn't help but feel some hope. Perhaps this man could help me. His strength was evident in muscular arms, despite his age. Perhaps that strength gave him favor with the ancestors and they would bring healing to my joints.

The healer continued, slanting his head towards Uncle Steven. "When will his father come?"

Uncle Steven explained about my father's trip and the uncertainty of its length. Christine agreed to stay with me and care for me as we waited. Uncle Steven left, telling us that he would direct Daddy to where I was.

Over the next few days, my condition worsened. I grew weaker and could do nothing for myself. Lifting me to the latrine was not easy for Christine.

During this time, I noticed a strange thing. I never saw Mulego walk. At night, he somehow slipped into his bedroom, but we did not see him go. And the next morning, he would suddenly be sitting on the cow hide carpet. How did he move so quickly? I assumed that my haze of fever made me less aware. But Christine noticed also.

One day, Christine came into the hut after trading for some food with a neighbor. "I have solved the mystery," she whispered. "The neighbors say Mulego cannot walk!"

Cannot walk? How then could this healer make me stand again if the ancestors had not listened to him about his own legs?

The neighbors told Christine that none of them saw him walk, but neither did they see how he managed to move from one place to another. All his supplies were brought to him at his hut so that he did not need to travel.

Daddy finally arrived a week after my sickness began. His expression at seeing his son so ill made my heart hurt along with my joints.

"My son!" he cried. "What a critical condition you are in!"

He greeted Mulego with a hug, and they sat down to talk over the milk Christine brought in.

"I can help your son," Mulego stated in a superior tone. "If I am successful, you must give me a cow. If I bring great results for your son, then we will negotiate further payment."

Daddy closed his eyes, nodding already. "Yes, yes. If you need more than one cow, it is fine. Just help my son. Please."

The knowing gaze of the healer did not comfort me. Did not Daddy tell me to never barter this way? You must pretend you do not want the item, then try to lower the price. Never agree to more. What was he thinking? The worry tired my sick body, and I dozed during their conversation.

The next morning, before dawn, Daddy came to say goodbye, as he must retrieve a cow and his business dealings could wait no longer. His face was barely visible in the dim light of the paraffin candle. I clutched his hand, as my fingers were the only joints that felt normal, and he squeezed mine back. As sick as I was, we did not know if we would meet again. He asked Christine to stay with me so I would not be entirely alone. Through the door of the hut, I watched Daddy pedal away, disappearing into the darkened jungle.

Mulego twisted around from where he sat and retrieved something. The flame of the candle struck a gleaming knife in his hand. "We will begin now."

He ordered Christine outside, and we were alone. "Give me your knee," he ordered. "Dawn comes only once each day."

My body was too weak to resist, though I wished I could slide my body away from him. When I didn't move, he yanked my leg toward him, and I screamed. Next, I felt a sharp pain on the top of my knee.

"Ow!" I shouted, "you cut me!"

"Quiet, boy," he rasped. "Your father has promised to pay me well, and I have promised to help you." He reached one hand to a shelf and selected a green leaf. He squeezed my knee hard and smeared the blood on the leaf's surface.

Leaning forward until his face filled my vision, he held my gaze for an eternal moment. "Let me be clear. You will do what I say, when I say, with no complaining. I will not fail, and you will walk. Your pitiful cries mean nothing to me. Only my success."

The drawing of blood occurred again and again, always at dawn and at sunset. Mulego cut my knees, waist, and bottom. I had no idea of the significance of my blood on a leaf, but the blood seemed to tell him something about what treatment I needed and how long it would last. He also smeared vile-smelling herbal pastes on my overheated skin.

But worse than all those things was the 'cure' for my weakened limbs.

Mulego made Christine lift me high in the hut and told me to grab the pillars supporting the roof. Though my hands were not affected by the polio, my elbows and shoulders were inflamed. As soon as Christine let go, the weight of my body hung from my elbows and shoulders. I immediately fell to the dirt floor, screaming at the jolt.

The healer grabbed me roughly. "You will hang, and this will make you strong once more. Don't you want to walk again? Get up. Lift your hands once more."

My sobs were reduced to whimpers from fear and exhaustion. I fell a second time. His face contorted with anger, and I believed he wanted to hit me.

"This boy must strengthen his legs," he growled. "Make him hold the roof beams until his toes just touch the floor. If he starts to slip, you must hold him there."

Christine nodded, some of my own fear reflecting in her eyes. She obeyed without question, though I thought I detected pity in her expressions.

I knew I was in big trouble with this man, yet I was so thankful for Christine. However, the healer greatly intimidated my stepmother, so that she was afraid to say anything to him about how he treated me. She believed him to be a great healer, and who could question a man of his stature? I overheard him tell her strongly that sympathy would only delay my recovery. Sometimes I saw tears on her cheeks when I cried in desperation, but she could not intervene.

"Hold on, Canisius. You can do it. I believe these treatments will help you," she whispered to me one night. "Perhaps this will only be for a little while longer." But I saw resignation in her eyes, and each time she saw me, she cried.

Christine could not be with me at every moment, and the healer had to see other patients who came to him for treatment. On those occasions, he tied my wrists to the ceiling or to a tree with ropes, and I hung there for hours alone.

Through the bleak, sleepless nights I longed for my mother, but she had returned to her family, leaving my little sister Catrine in the village with my other siblings. I longed for the hospital, where the doctors didn't guess at treatments. I longed for Daddy to come and save me. There was no use in prayer to God. He seemed to have no use for me.

Weeks passed, and I became despondent. I came to believe that Mulego had no idea how to help me. That the ancestors were not listening to him. That God had abandoned me. I could not move myself around. Could not sit up by myself. Christine had to do everything for me. If I lived through this, what kind of future could I look forward to?

One day I overheard Mulego talking to Christine as they sat outside in the shade of the hut. "I will try one more thing, and then I may be forced to abandon my goal." Someone coughed, and a rooster crowed in the yard. "I expected him to die from the start. I wish I could have made progress to receive the cow."

And so came the injections. The healer said they were to reduce my fever. When Uncle Steven came to visit, Mulego sent him to purchase the medicine and the syringe.

The needle seemed as large as my hand. I had no idea what the vial contained; all I knew was that the shot made me ache for hours, though tears refused to come from my dehydrated eyes.

In the dark moments of the night, I questioned God. Are you even there? Why has all this happened to me?

No answers came.

Finally, Daddy returned. The healer spoke to him gravely. "I have failed your son. Find another place. Take him somewhere else."

Mulego did not get his cow.

Abuse

MY HEART LONGED for home. For my own hut and my sleeping mat. For familiar faces of those who loved me as I died in peace.

But it was not to be.

Daddy knew of a more powerful traditional healer farther away, but he had not been here to choose the healer the first time. This one had the distinction of having my father's sister as his second wife, so Daddy had more trust in him. The distance was great—about sixty miles away, but he felt he had no choice but to make the journey. I resigned myself to another pain-filled bicycle ride.

My stepmother Christine joined us on the day-long bicycle trip to care for me when Daddy had to be gone. Poor Christine was worn out from caring for me by herself and needed the help of another woman. Thankfully, Maria and the

other women of my family took care of the chores back in the
village.

Strangely, I felt hope again. Perhaps this man knew
more rituals, different herbs. Since he was connected to us by
marriage, maybe our family's ancestral spirits respected him
more highly. And surely I would be treated with more care
and kindness than before.

The sun was setting when we arrived in a jungle
clearing. I had closed my eyes during the bumpy ride and
gritted my teeth against the agony in my joints. When I
opened my eyes, three huts stood before us. The first and
largest, I found out later, belonged to the healer's first wife,
the second belonged to my aunt, and the third housed the
older children of the first wife. In the background sat several
storage buildings and a chicken house. The compound was
surrounded by a tall fence to keep the cows away from the
huts. Everything looked familiar, not so different from my
village at home.

The healer, whose name was Nakisisa, greeted us. His
eyes held a steady gaze and his mouth did not smile. He
appeared shorter than Mulego, though I had never seen that
healer stand. At least this healer could walk on his own.
Nakisisa's skin was light, and his brown eyes took in
everything. He wore trousers, unlike Mulego. The two

healers were different in so many ways. In my mind, that was a very good thing.

He and Daddy clasped arms together and hugged, and the sight made my heart glad. Treatment from someone known by my family would be so much better, I reasoned.

Daddy explained my condition.

"You say he has fever?" Nakisisa's gentle voice surprised me and gave me comfort. I wished I had come to him from the start. "Then there is great hope. Everyone knows that while the fever rages, the polio can be treated. After the fever leaves, there is no more hope."

In a loud voice, the healer declared, "In one week, this young man will be walking."

Encouragement flooded my heart. One week! Perhaps I could return to school before long. Though I still shivered from extreme chills, I tried to smile.

Daddy spoke with him about payment. I felt so much love for him. He had worked so hard for years to change our family's financial condition. He had done everything he could to save my life since the snakebite, the measles, and now the polio. Yet he was willing to pay all he had to be sure I could walk again. Saying goodbye to him was very hard for me.

Nakisisa woke me early the next morning while it was still dark. He carried me outside and set me down. Soon after, a man arrived on a bicycle to pick up milk.

"Do you see that man?" Nakisisa said, pointing. "He was once a patient of mine. He could not walk, and I helped him. You are going to be all right." His bushy brows furrowed. "You see, he was much worse than you."

Truly, my hopes soared, and I felt ready for the wonderful treatments that would cause me to walk in the next week. Daddy had said goodbye and already pedaled away, but I was determined the next time he saw me, I would greet him standing on my own two feet.

When dawn came soon after, Nakisisa said it was time for the first treatment. My heart sank when I spotted a razor in his hand.

Well, I told myself, maybe some of the rituals are the same, but others will be different. I gritted my teeth through the slice of the blade, and breathed through my mouth when he applied smelly herbal pastes to my skin.

Next, he had Christine carry my limp form over to the fence on the edge of the clearing. A churning feeling began in my stomach. Surely not—

"Boy, you will hold on to this fence with your toes touching the ground. If we do this often enough, you will walk in one week."

Nakisisa cast a stern look at my stepmother and aunt. "I caution you both to show no mercy or sympathy. This will only serve to make the boy lazy. The medicine I use is powerful, and I will allow no interference."

Both women nodded, admiration and fear in their eyes.

The fever had wasted my strength severely over the last month, and I had no voice to protest that this method had failed miserably. He would not have listened anyway. For I realized that like the first healer, his eyes looked for the cows he might earn from a man like my daddy. My newfound hope drained away like water in a leaky bucket.

And so I found myself hanging again—just from a different place this time.

Dog

"I CAN NOT do this any longer," I whispered to Christine one night. My throat was hoarse from crying due to the unrelenting pain, which was terrible enough without having to hang from a fence. "I feel I will die."

"Be strong, Canisius," Christine wiped my feverish brow with a cool cloth dipped in river water. "Your daddy trusts this healer. Christine trusts this healer. And I trust him, too. He can be the one to bring results."

But that was a false hope. Nakisisa made me stand for hours longer than the first healer, and due to their respect and trust, Christine was unwilling to bring any objection to his methods. Many times, the healer warned Christine to stay away from me. Since the two of them could not be with me always, I was vulnerable to whatever someone wanted to do.

His arguments with them were very convincing—that he was doing the right thing, and their presence might hinder how his medicine worked. And he was very good at intimidation.

"He will not get well if you coddle him!" Nakisisa said sternly.

Christine dared to ask. "Who will lift him when he falls?"

"I have someone to take care of that," he replied.

And he did.

Though I stayed in the hut with Nakisisa's second wife, my auntie, his adult daughter, Lwango, from his first wife lived in the last hut with the other older children. The first time I met her, I thought she could be a beautiful woman, except for the scowl on her face. The traumas of life had taken the joy from this woman. In my early days at the traditional healer's compound, I learned to identify Lwango's strident voice, and auntie told me a little about her.

"She was married for some time, but her husband divorced her," auntie whispered one evening. "He sent her home, and the shame has made her already troublesome personality even worse. Avoid her if you can."

Sadly, I could do no such thing, for the traditional healer asked Lwango to check on me through the day.

My days followed a similar schedule. At dawn, Nakisisa would come and cut me to determine some hidden knowledge about how to treat me. That blade caused me so much fear and agony. After this, I would lie exhausted, watching the sunrise until someone carried me to the latrine. Sitting up on my own was impossible. Food did not interest me. All I wanted to do was sleep.

However, just as the sun began to beat down with intensity, that was the time Nakisisa felt was best for me to hang from the fence. He or Lwango hung me in place. The hanging lasted for hours—however many the healer had determined from my blood that morning. Then at sundown, he would cut me again.

And the next day repeated the nightmare.

When I was hanging, the pain in my joints was more than I could bear. The fatigue beyond my comprehension. I cried. I yelled. I sobbed. I called out, "Why will my family refuse to help me?"

The helpless feeling reminded me of the lonely nights when I suffered from the snakebite, and there was no one to do anything for me. Why am I here? I cried. Death, come and take me. Even death is better than this suffering.

Every morning, Lwango hung me on the fence. "You had better hold on to the branches today. I will be angry with you if you let go."

My constant fever and the illness eating at my nerves and joints left me weaker each day. When she lectured me and stared into my eyes, my spirit melted, because I knew my hands could not support my body weight for long.

The sun beat down, yet I shivered. I tried to distract myself by listening to bird calls and the dogs barking, but my sweating hands began to slip. Though the feel of my stretched joints was extreme, the thought of my body hitting the hard-packed ground was far, far worse. I began to cry long before my hands let go of their own accord. And always, I knew the inevitable awaited. I would fall down. The weakness of fever and dehydration, the agony and inflammation of my joints, or the strength of the sun—all these conspired to keep me from clinging to the fence.

The niggling thought always started first. "My hands are slipping. Hold on!" My heartbeat increased, and I struggled for a better grip, despite my sweaty fingers. Then my mind would begin to imagine the fire of the impact of my body hitting the dirt. Sweat from fear dripped from my temples into my eyes. But I had no free hand to wipe it away.

Meanwhile, during my agonized anticipation, I usually heard Lwango's voice. She argued with everyone. Her brothers, her sister, and most of all, her mother. Auntie had said that a person bitter about their situation, sometimes abuses whoever or whatever is near, like slamming a door or kicking a dog.

And I was Lwango's dog.

Each moment I heard her quarrel with someone, I nearly let go of the fence in fright, because I knew what came next. I could only hold myself to the fence for so long, and then I would fall. But the pain of that collapse was nothing to what always followed. Sometimes I had an hour to lay there, panting, trying to regain my strength. Sometimes, I only had a minute. For Lwango would come charging at me, usually from behind, so I could not prepare myself. She stopped to stare in disgust when she saw my crumpled form in the dirt. "How dare you disobey my father! He is a great healer. You have no desire to get well!" she screamed.

Lwango grabbed a stout stick—a thick, knotty branch that she kept nearby just for these moments, and she began to beat me, calling me names and shaming me. Pounding my body, flailing my eight-year-old frame in her frustration.

My aching joints vibrated with each strike, and I thought over and over again, "I cannot endure anymore."

"Why must you fail again and again? My father is a great man, doing his best to make you well. And you can not even try to do as he asks. Get up! You will hang longer this time!"

The level of her anger made it seem as though I had injured her badly. I could not understand the reason for her hatred. God, what did I do to deserve this treatment? In my heart, I began to hate her.

This treatment occurred every day, multiple times each day. The beatings left swollen lumps all over my body. They throbbed all night long.

My only source of solace during this time was from Nakisisa's son. He was perhaps fifteen or sixteen, and he showed me love and kindness. His gentle smile was like a ray of sunshine in a dark pit. He tried to tell his sister not to hurt me, but she would not listen to anyone. I developed such fear of Lwango, that just the thought of her in my dreams made me cry.

Eventually, the healer constructed a wooden frame for me to hang on instead of the fence. When I hung from the frame each day, even when I knew Lwango was away at some task in the jungle, my mind chanted, she is coming, she is coming. I shivered even in the sticky, shimmering air.

Did I hear a scuffle in the dirt behind me? She liked to sneak up and catch me. My anger began to turn to bitterness.

The promised week had long since passed, with no improvement at all. Weeks turned into a month, and still I remained there. I turned my thoughts inward. "God doesn't know me. He cares nothing for me. Why do they have to beat me with canes, when my body will not have the strength for what they say I must do?"

When the rains came, they took me inside the hut to hang from the support poles. Being out of the hot sun was a relief, and for some reason I did not have to hang as long inside. Each day I prayed for rain, and when rain began, I felt as if it were a miracle.

My abusive treatment continued into the second month, and then a third. One day, Lwango brought Nakisisa to me after I had fallen from the frame yet again. "Do you see how he disrespects me, father? He will not stay standing, no matter how I punish him."

Nakisisa set his hands on his hips. "Perhaps you wish to make me look foolish for your father when he returns. Your cries must be pretense, for you do not stand, even when beaten with sticks." He pursed his lips, thinking. "Perhaps you need more reason to stand. If you don't stand there, we will not take you to the toilet."

I felt as though my heart dropped to the ground, trampled under his feet as he strode away. Lwango twisted her lips at me, gloating.

A heavy downpour began again, and Lwango grudgingly carried me into the hut to hang, as the branches were too slick in the rain. On a normal day, she would have stopped for me to use the latrine, but this time she just slowed as she walked past, as if to make her father's point. She set me up in the hut, and I made a resolution in my heart.

"I will not eat again, or drink again, so I will not need the latrine. No matter how parched my throat, I will not be tempted."

My hands turned pale from the lack of circulation, and I knew they would soon let go. I stared at the floor, dreading the coming impact. And then, of course, it came. I tried to keep from crying out, alerting Lwango that it was time to beat me. My whimpers stayed quiet, as I tried to catch my breath. I had no strength in my back or my limbs to even readjust myself to a comfortable position, so I just lay there, dreading my tormentor's return.

Only a little time passed before my bowels began to complain. Due to the illness and lack of appetite, my stools were difficult to hold back. I swallowed hard and focused on a fly buzzing around the hut. Watching the insect circle with such freedom increased my discouragement.

The pressure in my gut turned to pain. If only Christine were here today, she would carry me to the toilet! But she had traveled to a nearby village to purchase food for us. I was alone.

Finally, I knew I could last no longer. The agony made me cry silently in my heart. I used my right hand, lying near my knee, to pull my knee an inch toward the door. Next, my left hand dragged my left knee. Then I pressed both palms to the floor in order to shift my body to catch up to my legs. Pain shrieked from every joint.

Time passed slowly, and my movements were incremental. Making my way just a few feet to the door sapped my strength, yet my bodily functions still screamed for attention. At long last, I was able to clear the door. However, I knew I would never make the journey all the way to the latrine on the other side of the clearing. I barely managed to slide my shorts down before my body demanded attention. I felt buried in shame. How had I come to this?

And that was where Lwango found me, filthy and sapped of energy.

The expression on her face frightened me, even before I heard her voice. Her jaw clenched and her nostrils flared. A growl came from her throat before words. "How dare you repay our generosity with this mess?" she spat out. "My father told you that without hanging, there would be no visits to the toilet. You will be sorry for the mess you made."

She did make me sorry. But not even the pain of those sticks on my ravaged joints eclipsed the shame that scarred my soul. I cried out to God. "Help me or let me die."

My aunt arrived that evening. She frowned at the new bumps on my body. My food sat untouched beside me.

"Why did you not eat today, Canisius?"

"Oh Auntie, I wish to die. They won't take me to the toilet, and I made a mess. I can't repeat that." She held me as I sobbed into her shoulder. My aunt cried, too.

Daddy came soon after that. He and Uncle Steven had found a ride in a car to visit me.

The healer greeted them, then folded his arms and spoke slowly. "I have helped many, but I have failed your son. Take him home and wait for the day he will die. There is no treatment left. He will not survive."

I had barely survived almost three months with the second traditional healer and his daughter. Was there any hope for me?

The tears on Daddy's face said 'no'. Always before, he determined to find a way to help. Now, after so many illnesses, and so many treatments, I knew he was giving up.

Adventure

I RETURNED HOME a nine-year-old cripple. My shriveled legs caused people to stare. On the inside I felt that the boy who ran fast, the boy who climbed trees, the boy who made his father proud, had disappeared into the pain. I was nowhere to be found. No one saw me—the true me.

The journey home was not easy. Since Daddy and Uncle Steven did not know I would be discharged that day, they had not brought the bicycle. The only way to travel the sixty-some miles home was on foot. Daddy, Uncle Steven, Christine and my aunt took turns carrying me, trekking through the jungle and taking every shortcut they knew. The trip stretched the entire day from early morning to evening. Every step jolted white-hot spears through my joints.

When we reached the village, the whole family came out to greet me. But instead of smiles and joy, hopelessness and despair filled their eyes. If the healer said there was no solution, no one else had any idea what to do for me. As soon as they saw me, they wailed as if I had already died. I suppose that was true in one way. The venomous snakebite should have killed me. The infection of measles weakened me. But pain from the polio was the hardest of all because it stopped life. It stopped everything.

This was such a trying time for me. The only thing I could do physically was lie flat. With no strength in my back, I could not sit by myself. Someone had to support me even for sitting, and then only with my legs straight out in front of me. My knee joints were too painful to bend. No matter where I needed to go, I had to be carried or lifted. I felt useless and ashamed.

When people saw me, they cried to see such a twisted husk of a boy. I not only grieved the physical abilities my illness had taken from me, but I also grieved the loss of my ability to make people happy. No one smiled at me anymore. No one thanked me for helping with chores or with the children. I no longer had a purpose.

The boy who wanted to be somebody was now a nobody.

Months passed, and I was determined to at least learn to move a little bit. My joints still screamed at me, but I clenched my teeth and bent my protesting knees a little further each day. Learning to maneuver would take longer.

Despite all this, I tried to tell myself to stay positive. I still didn't know what my purpose in life could be. I no longer thought I could be somebody. But as long as I was alive, I could try to make my back, legs, and arms a little stronger, and that gave me purpose. I didn't know where my will to try came from. Maybe it was from the joy I felt when five-year-old Catrine came by to prattle and play with me. Oh, how much I loved my little sister!

I began to think of this time as a 'new adventure in a new world'. I made it a goal—like a game—to see how far I could progress each week. The initial healing process dragged on for over a full year, with pain and stiff joints the worst symptoms. Even one year after contracting polio, I still felt pain, though not as extreme.

The interior of the hut was chilly, but I did not want to bother people to carry me out into the sunshine. I practiced dragging my folded body short distances, trying to build strength into my wasted spine. But the improvements came slowly. I felt like an inchworm with a mountain to climb.

After that first year, I was still in a tough place. Though I could drag myself a little, sitting on my own was still a problem. Sometimes, after working myself into a sitting position, my weakened back would give way and I would topple over. After many months of determined work, I was able to sit by myself, leaning against the wall, of course. Sitting had taken me a full year to master.

1988 brought another loss. Catrine was taken away. One of my aunts, who lived in a village in Rwanda, came to visit. Aunt Nzamugura fell in love with five-year-old Catrine's sunny personality. Though she had a large family back in Rwanda, she longed to bring a piece of her Ugandan family home with her. Daddy agreed to let Catrine go.

Sadness settled on me like a dark raincloud. I could not shake the heaviness of losing my sister. Was not the loss of Mama enough? The loss of my mobility? Did I have to lose Catrine too? My bitterness and anger at God increased, smoldering through my soul like green leaves on fire.

During the next year, I developed the ability to heave myself short distances, pulling myself along with my arms, while my legs dragged behind me. This was a great victory, but it came with a cost. As I pulled myself along, rocks and thorns ripped at the skin of my legs and palms. Mud smeared into those wounds, causing infection.

Eventually, I was able to coax my joints into kneeling. This was the first step in being able to crawl—but that would not happen for some time. My spine remained weak and shaky, but kneeling felt like a great achievement. I was also able to scoot backward on my bottom in order to travel to the latrine, or from hut to hut. This method was not fast but helped to keep my legs and arms mud-free. The downside to scooting on my bottom were the holes I wore through my shorts. I was ashamed of my shabbiness.

My days were full of boredom, as there was nothing useful I could do. It was not easy to hold things in my hands—perhaps due to the strain of hanging for months when I was with the traditional healers. Time ticked by like slow dripping honey.

One day, a man come to our village. He opened his sack and set up an area to work. He began to fashion needles, arrows, and knives. Family members purchased these items from him or traded for them. He sharpened metal for knives, and melted rubber or plastic for the handles. I watched him for a long time and made a decision. I would teach myself to do these sorts of things. If I strengthened my hands, I could make a living someday, and have a purpose for my life.

I began to practice with small items around our house and from things people brought me. Some of my efforts were failures, but slowly my abilities improved. With plastic or rubber, I fashioned knife handles. I learned how to sharpen the metal. I crafted needles and arrowheads. Soon, family members came to me for items they needed. In addition to these skills, I also learned how to cut hair. My brothers and sisters would sit down on the ground so I could reach them. Eventually other family members sought me out to trim their hair. I was happy to have these skills and they gave purpose to my days.

But my new-found skills did not change the fact that I was disabled. The hopes and dreams that my father had for me were gone. I could read the grief and sorrow in his face when he looked at me. This knowledge flowed through the deep places of my heart, like a dark river rushing beneath steep banks.

At night, I delayed going to bed, because sleep could not find me. I lay on my grass mattress and reviewed the hurtful things people had said about me that day. I would cry for hours. I was looking for someone to blame for my troubles, my pain, my disappointment. I wanted to know that my life was not a waste, that I could still have purpose and meaning in spite of all my suffering.

That pain in my heart turned to anger. Anger turned to bitterness. And bitterness sometimes gave way to hatred. Mostly hatred at God, the one who could have made things different for me.

Mobility

IN THE FALL of 1989, I was stronger and finally achieved a great goal—crawling on my hands and knees. This victory had taken me two and a half years to learn.

Despite my advancement, I continued to feel discouraged by how my family viewed me. They did not say how proud they were of me. They were not as willing to help me, and I could see their eyes skip past me as if I was not there—as if I was nothing. I knew deep down they loved me, but my situation was too hard for them. No one else in our family—or our entire area—had a disability, so dealing with someone like me was unfamiliar.

I heard in my mind, "You are nothing. Helpless. Useless. No one loves you. No one cares about you."

When my friends ran past, kicking the football or having a race, I pasted a smile on my face and pretended that my awkward, jerky movements did not bother me. But my smile fell away as soon as they were out of sight.

During this time, Daddy moved our village and herd to the district of Luwero, and now we lived near a larger town called Bululi. He had been spying out this area at the time I developed polio, due to the over-grazing in our other area, but waited until my recovery stabilized somewhat before making the move to Luwero. The grass near our old village had become over-grazed, and the cows were not producing enough milk.

On the journey to our new home, I saw something strange and wonderful—a small bicycle with three wheels instead of two. My eyes followed this new vehicle with hunger. If only my legs were strong enough to pedal such a contraption. What freedom I would have! But Daddy's delay in moving the family while I recovered had set us in an unfavorable place financially. Even if we could afford such an extravagance, my legs would not make it work. But the seed was planted—wheels could mean freedom.

In our new home, my family began attending the Catholic church, as it was close by and most others in the area went also. Sundays became lonely when everyone went to services without me. Although they attended regularly, they did not believe in the Christian God.

At Christmas, Daddy sold a cow and bought clothes and shoes for everybody. It seemed to me that everyone attended church just to show off their new clothes. The holiday and Daddy's kindness towards my family brought me more heartache. Because I was now a cripple, I had no need for new shoes. I pretended not to care. Daddy sent a cow for slaughter and shared meat with our neighbors, but inside, my soul withered. Christmas brought me no joy.

Sometimes, some 'born-again' Christians came to our village to preach to me about God, but I ignored them. Had not God ignored me? I wished with all my heart that I could ask God my questions. If he didn't answer to my satisfaction, I was willing to go into the boxing ring and fight him. Such was my frustration--and my ignorance.

To make matters worse, the school in our new area was within walking distance for the children in our village. My brothers and sister excitedly prepared for the new school term. But not me.

When you have a physical disability, people assume that your intelligence is affected as well. No one thought about the possibility of school for me.

I watched from the corner of my eye as Joseph, Janet, and even my younger brother Sunday walked, tall and proud, on the path to the school. A path I could no longer travel.

Unlimited

I tried to focus on gratitude that I was no longer at the mercy of the traditional healers, but it was not easy. I now understood Lwango's hatred and bitterness, and wondered if the same feelings would infect my soul and fester there like the wounds on my legs.

When everyone returned from school, holding real books and paper, I longed to turn the pages for myself. Perhaps I might remember the letter sounds from my few months of school over two years ago.

I reached for Joseph's book sitting on a stool.

"Hands off!" Joseph shouted, snatching the book before I touched it. "Look at you. You are filthy. You will dirty the pages of my schoolbook."

Janet nodded in agreement, and even Sunday slid his books behind his back.

I looked down at myself. "You are right," I whispered. "I am dirty." I always tried to be as clean as I could, but there was no way to keep my hands dirt-free in order to touch those white pages. Being forced to drag myself through the inevitable mud of the long rainy season left its mark. I longed to look clean and neat, but my movement on the ground prevented that.

I made my way to the bucket and washed myself off. But by the time I finished, bleakness consumed me. My siblings made sure to keep their school things out of my reach after that.

My family and others assumed that because my legs didn't work, that I could not feel wounds. The polio took my strength, not my ability to feel. Each time I crawled, I felt dirt and gravel grinding into scratches. Naturally, they developed infections, and my hands endured the same abuse without any protection.

At times, I tried to bend my knees above and behind my neck and walk only on my hands to reduce the impact on my legs. This was especially helpful when it rained, as my legs stayed cleaner. But again, shame came into the equation. I felt as if I looked like an insect, and I resorted to this method only when it was dark, and no one could see.

When my back strengthened a little more, my brother, Sunday, would hold my legs in his hands so that I could 'walk' like a wheelbarrow. We could not go far in this way, but I asked Sunday to help me when the wounds on my legs were especially painful.

One bright spot during this time was that I continued my practice of helping toddlers to walk. Aunt Prisca bore a second son to Uncle Steven, by the name of Thomas Mugabo.

Whenever I crawled somewhere, Thomas crawled over and grabbed onto my shirt and pulled himself to standing. He held on so tight as he balanced on his feet. When I moved forward, he made a shaky step also. After several weeks, he began to walk by himself.

Another little cousin, Ncuruza, was also learning to walk at this time. We made a comical sight, with one baby on my left, and one on my right, and me crawling in the middle. We were forced to stop often as Mugabo and Ncuruza became jealous of one another, both claiming me for their own.

I loved those little boys with all my heart. They did not see me as a disabled person, but someone who was useful, someone who made them happy. Even from an early age, I loved young children. I had dreamed that one day I would marry, and have many children. My current reality looked bleak in that regard. Girls my age would come to the village. I had reached the time that their beautiful faces and slender forms attracted my attention. But how could any of them ever want me for a husband? One who could not provide. One with holes in his shorts. One with no education.

Like a kettle building with steam, anger continued filling me. Anger towards the traditional healers, towards those who did not help me or see me, and towards a God who did not care.

Spirits

GOD WAS COMPLICATED. Rwandan people have always believed in one supreme God, who was all-powerful. But to speak with him, you had to go through channels such as mediums and witch doctors. They could connect to the ancestral spirits, who could then connect with God.

In Bululi, the spiritual influence was much stronger than before. From what I understood, even the Catholic church had channels to God. They had different spirits, called saints. Not so different from our cultural beliefs. Just different rituals.

I was beginning to understand that there seemed to be two spiritual forces at work in our lives. One was for our good, and the other was dark and harmful.

When anything out of the ordinary happened, our family viewed this as something bad. We then had to go and consult the witch doctors to discern what we should do.

I remember meeting many different witch doctors. Their rituals varied. Some studied the fats from a slaughtered animal, which somehow gave the witch doctor information about what we were supposed to do. Others used knucklebones, tossing them and studying how they landed. Some burned incense. We even sang songs for the spirits.

All of the things involving spirits made me uncomfortable. When we visited a place where the spirits were, the witch doctors made sure it was dark. These huts had no windows. When we went inside, we knew we were no longer in control. The witch doctors managed everything, scaring us by speaking in different voices.

One incident that shook me was when our friend's aunt died. The witch doctor explained that the aunt was not pleased. "Your family has not made the right sacrifices on her behalf. Go and find someone who has never had contact with your aunt."

The woman they found, a stranger to me, sat in the middle of the darkened hut. The witch doctor pulled out the horn of a buffalo. In a deep voice, he began to sing, calling that spirit. Summoning it forth.

And the spirit came.

The woman, eyes glazed, opened her mouth and spoke. Gooseflesh raised on my arms.

She spoke with the dead aunt's voice.

The same tone, the same way of expression, as if she were still alive. I felt shivers in my soul. I knew these spirits were real.

Another time, I saw a man attacked by spirits. His body shook violently and was thrown here and there on the ground. Several people had to sit on him to hold him down.

And I have even seen spirits kill people. If someone wanted revenge, they could consult the witch doctor to have the spirits attack another person. I have seen people who were healthy one moment drop dead when the spirits came upon them.

The worst events I witnessed were during funerals. These were sad times to say goodbye to friends and relatives. But in the Bululi area, they could become terrifying.

Sometimes, the witch doctors called down cannibalistic spirits who would manifest in some of the funeral guests. These guests would leap into the grave, and begin to gnaw the dead body. The person did not want to do this, but the spirits forced them to do so. The sight of this stirred great fear in my heart.

In light of all my hardships, I wanted to please the spirits to prevent more bad things from happening to me.

Spirits were not personal. They were entities to be feared. We lived our lives to appease them. They could harm us, and were never encountered as a blessing or good fortune. You didn't make friends with a spirit, you could not know them. You only saw their effects when they were displeased.

This was in such contrast to the Christian God. I was greatly perplexed when I heard from born-again Christians that God, the Supreme Spirit, not only knew me but that he loved me. That this God did not intend to harm me, but instead desired to bless me. How could any of that be true about a spirit?

I already decided that God hated me, since he had allowed my life to become such a nightmare. Why had no one else in my family been bitten by a puff adder? Why had none of my friends contracted measles or polio? Seeing others healthy and carefree was a great injustice to me.

I did not understand these injustices. I did not understand how a spirit could be loving or personal. I did not understand how a spirit did not wand to harm me but instead to bless me. Who was this spirit—this God I did not know?

Darkness

THE VILLAGE DOGS set to barking, their growls and yips vibrating through the sticky afternoon. Excited greetings for the visitor echoed from the women outside, and a sour feeling grew in my stomach.

Visitors came time and time again, and always the same things happened.

In the scant moments before our neighbor, Mugisa, entered Maria's hut, I sprang into action—as much as a cripple could. I gripped my withered calves with aching fingers and bent my rusted knees. I pulled against a stool until my upper legs folded against my chest. Then I scooted myself and my mat inch by painful inch so that I leaned myself against the wall.

If only the color of my skin could match the dried mud walls, I might have my wish—invisibility.

By the time Mugisa entered our hut, I appeared just as I wanted—a youth, resting in his hut, perhaps waiting for the hottest part of the day to pass. But in the depths of my heart, I knew better. Everyone knew my story. I was the only disabled person for many villages around. A novelty. An oddity. Someone to be pitied.

With more warning, I could have struggled to the latrine and back, but now I was stuck. Why, oh why, had I finished off that cup of milk? For however long Mugisa sat telling stories with my father, asking after each others' families, and eventually coming around to the business of bartering, I would be held captive. Our social ritual was to offer milk, then a smoke, then alcohol. An eternity!

For nothing would persuade me to move. Not heat or exhaustion. Not aching hunger, burning thirst, cramping muscles, nor a straining bladder. Having to be seen moving by my family was embarrassing enough. But for others to watch me drag myself was the epitome of shame.

Mugisa's visit stretched on. Daddy invited him to stay for dinner, and my eyes closed in weary resignation. At last, my bladder, which had been needling me for hours, screamed and I was forced to move. I painstakingly rearranged my limbs in order to drag my resistant body out to the latrine.

With every awkward slide across the floor, I worried that my bladder would release, and my shame would be magnified.

During the long journey, the man stopped his incessant chatter and watched with unveiled curiosity. As I slowly inched out the door, Mugisa's voice rang behind me. He did not even try to keep quiet.

"He was such a good boy. A son his father could be proud of. It would be better for that one to be dead. He should not make everyone so sad to see him. You should give him some poison and end his misery."

I navigated in slow motion around the mud puddles that littered the compound between me and the destination I needed so badly. The man's words rang through my mind like the echoes of a monkey's cry in the jungle. He was right, of course. He was just voicing what my whole family—the entire village—probably thought, even if they did not say it out loud. I felt that this man truly understood my desperate circumstance.

Some visitors cried over me. Some just stared. Some said I should have died. They spoke about me as if I could not hear their hurtful words. These comments made me feel so small. Made me want to sit still as a rock so no one would notice me. Made me wonder—would I bring sadness to people for the rest of my life?

"God, if you are even there," I said, "why me?"

When Mugisa finally rose to take his leave, he walked over to where I sat and gazed down at me for a long moment. "You have great sadness, I can see." He lifted his chin and held two fingers to his lips. "Here is some advice. Take up smoking. It will reduce your sorrow."

I blinked in surprise as he left, wondering if he spoke the truth. Shrugging my shoulders, I determined to give smoking a try. Perhaps it would help.

I convinced neighbors and friends to give me cigarettes, though I never let Daddy see me smoking. Smoking was illegal for young people at that time. Smoking at least gave me something to do, even if it did nothing for my depression. I only gained an addiction.

And I had another reason to hang my head. Maria passed away that year. Her iron spirit and tenacity would be missed, and we all grieved. Mama even came all the way from her home for the funeral. At the time, I did not know that I would not see Mama for ten more long years. Had I known, I would have clung to her.

Maria had been the guiding influence over our family rituals and witch doctor consultations, but after her passing, those traditions began to change. More of the family started going to the Catholic church, and not just on Christmas. One of my aunts, Jane, became a born-again Christian and traveled some distance to a different church in our area.

The new year of 1990 brought more changes. My siblings started another year of school without me, I gained another half-sibling through Christine, and Daddy married again. His third wife, Josephine Ntawiha seemed kind, but like everyone else did not expect anything good to become of me. Daddy decided to give each of his wives their own area and divide his herd of cows between them. Christine moved to Gayaza, about one hundred miles away, while I stayed in Bululi. I missed Christine a great deal. My birthday that July was my twelfth, and it seemed as though there was nothing to celebrate.

1990 also marked the beginning of conflict back in Rwanda. The Hutu-led government was opposed by Tutsi refugees, like my parents, who had fled Hutu violence against them in the past. Some Tutsi had found refuge in Uganda, and formed the Rwandan Patriotic Front, or RPF, to oppose the present Rwandan government. Though the conflict seemed far away, my youngest sister Catrine's well-being was always in the front of my mind, and I worried about her. I had not seen her in two years.

This was such a dark time for me, and I held God responsible.

I continued making knife handles and doing small tasks to show my family that I had potential. Sometimes, I asked, "Could I go to school?"

The answer was discouraging. "But there are no trade schools that teach sandal repair or shoe-shining." Ideas from other family members sounded worse. Begging in the streets. Weaving mats.

I wanted to cry out, "How will I be able to support myself? How would I ever be able to care for a wife or children? Would someone choose me?" The answer to the questions I was afraid to ask echoed through my soul.

Never.

Our family business was looking after cows. Herding them, milking them, protecting them. But without strong legs, this was impossible. No woman would care to marry me or believe in me, with no education and with the shameful way I was forced to move. And without a wife, there would be no children. The impossible longing caused my heart to break.

It is hard to believe in yourself if no one else believes in you.

No one suspected the agony roiling within me. I felt such guilt for burdening my family with my care and did not like to see them cry over me. So I pasted a smile on my face each morning, maintaining the facade of a happy person. But each night, I could contain my sadness no longer. Once I dragged myself to my bed, I curled up facing the wall and let loose all the tears that had gathered throughout the day.

But silently. Always silently.

Though the civil war in Uganda was over, and we no longer had issues with violent soldiers, still, the country experienced much insecurity and evil men took advantage of the situation to steal and kill. When thugs came to raid, as they sometimes did, it terrified me. The first and second time this happened, everyone scrambled to hide in the bush, and someone carried me along with them.

On this day, I sat, bored, in my stepmother's hut. No one talked to me. Nothing interested me. All I thought about was myself.

Suddenly, telltale gunshots tore through the humid air. Everyone screamed and scattered in the mad scramble to grab precious possessions and small children. But no one thought about me. I remained in the hut alone.

Realizing that no one was coming back for me, in a panic I crawled as fast as I could into the bush. The jungle on the edge of the clearing was not thick enough to hide me well. My heart pounded with fear as I heard the shouts and cries of the bandits come closer. My breath stopped as they ransacked the village, taking whatever they wanted. Would they find me? Could they hear my racing heart? Cold fear snaked down my backbone.

They did not see me, and finally left, for which I was thankful. But my family had not seen me either, which increased my depression. They took those who were important.

Lonely tears ran down my face. What kind of future stood before me, if situations like this continued? What if the conflict in Rwanda erupted here in Uganda? Who would take the time to carry me when soldiers came?

"Canisius," I told myself, "you don't deserve to live. Release your family from the burden. You are useless. Discover some means to take your life, and your family will feel relief."

In my heart, I came to the conclusion that my family had become tired of me. I was just a big burden to them, or they would not have overlooked me. I was not precious to anyone. If the soldiers had killed me, it would have been all right. Better even. My family no longer would have to look at me, care for me, or pity me.

My heart felt as hollow as a dried out gourd. But even a gourd was of far more use than someone like me.

I was expendable.

My family had no idea of my distress. I kept my emotions from my face. Everyone I knew had probably come to the same conclusion that I had no future.

Some people made things worse. "Canisius," they would say with a knowing expression. "Perhaps God knew you were going to become a bad person, so he let this happen to you."

Was this really true?

When I thought of bad people, thugs and raiding soldiers came to mind. I had always thought of them as bad men. Could God see something in my heart that would turn into such evil? I had always tried to be such a good boy, but I knew I was not perfect. I recognized the bitterness and hatred in my heart towards the healers who had abused me. My spirits sagged with despair at the thought of becoming like these bad men.

And voices accused me from within. You are useless. You don't matter to the family. You are different. Alone. You had better die.

Why not? The thought of death had flitted through my mind many times when my pain had been intense, but at those moments I lacked the strength or opportunity to act on my decision.

But now, I was stronger. And I had the advantage of invisibility. No one noticed when I went missing for a while. And by the time they thought to look for me, I would be dead. Free.

At first, I only thought about the idea of suicide, daydreaming about freedom from my lack of mobility and the stares directed my way. But before long, death became a constant thought. In my morbid fascination, I watched and waited for the perfect method and the right opportunity.

I glanced at my stepmother's favorite knife, boasting a handle I had fashioned myself. Perhaps it would be fitting to end my life with a tool I made with my own hands. I discarded the thought. Too messy. Despite how I was treated, I did not want my family to discover my bloody body.

I ticked through several options. Perhaps lying in the road to allow a truck to hit me. But traffic was sparse, and the deep ruts kept the vehicles' speeds too low to cause me damage.

Janet walked past our hut, balancing a saucepan of water on her head. I watched her graceful sway on strong legs, and a splash of water fell from the pot and darkened the dirt path. That was it! Drowning. That would not be messy

The river was too far for me. Maybe our well would do. I had to plan carefully so that my family would not notice and stop me. The well sat two entire kilometers away.

My plan was to leave just after the middle of the day. Water was collected in the morning, and by then the cows had already had their drink and were herded away. No one went to the well except morning and evening, due to fear of snakes.

Well, I had already been bitten by the snake, and if it happened again, I would let the venom take its course.

Six years ago when the snake bit me, a journey was required for me to live. Now, a journey was required for me to die.

Suicide

THE DAY FINALLY arrived. Daddy was away, as usual. That was a good thing, as his eyes missed nothing. Still, I would have liked to give him a hug as a way of saying goodbye. I loved Daddy deeply and wished to express my gratitude for all he had done for me. I hoped that he would not be full of guilt after my passing. I wished most of all for him to be relieved of the burden of a crippled son.

I waited until my stepmother was busy in the milk room, and told her I was going a little way into the jungle to collect grass for my bed. She nodded in a distracted way, and I crawled quickly over the threshold.

As fast as my arms could move, I headed for the cover of the bush, disregarding the roots and rocks I usually avoided. Once hidden from sight, I rested a moment, heart pounding like a beating drum. Then I took a deep breath and pushed on through thick brush and thorns. I did not dare take the path, as one of my family members might easily travel that way and ask where I was going.

With each foot I traveled, branches scratched at me and great roots seemed to rise up to block my way. Mud sucked at my knees, and thorns grabbed my already torn clothing as if trying to keep me from my mission.

Who had the power to do such a thing? Ancestral spirits? Bah. With all of my grandmother's sacrifices, prayers, and fetishes, her requests for me had not been answered.

That left God. If God was real, then he had power over the spirits. And if he had not ordered the spirits to help me in my distress, then that could mean only one thing—God despised me.

And no wonder. If my family had a hard time loving me, how much more so the supreme God? Surely he easily loved those who were beautiful and strong, who could do great things on his behalf. But not me.

Well, I decided, God would not come between me and the freedom I craved. I pushed on, determined, despite the pain, fatigue, and hunger. For in my haste to end my life, I had not considered that food might be necessary to accomplish my goal.

And so, nearly an hour later, I reached the well. To my relief, the well clearing was deserted. I lay panting for a long time, listening to parrots call back and forth, and took stock of my physical condition.

Hands—a throbbing mess of blisters and cuts. Knees—bruised and sore. Thighs and feet—scratched and bloody, just begging for further infection. The threads of my shirt and shorts barely held together, they were so tattered.

But none of those things mattered. Once free from this crippled body, what need had I for clothing? For smooth skin? The dead harbored no infection, needed no food. Longed for no love.

Yet, as my tongue stuck to the roof of my parched mouth, I was forced to admit my need for a drink. The anthill-shaped mud wall surrounding the well kept small children and animals from falling in, and would have to be scaled. Little of my energy remained for the task.

I dropped the rope with the gourd dipper into the depths of the well. It seemed an eternity of seconds passed before I heard the splash.

So. A long way down. That was good, I reassured myself. No second chances. No climbing out.

I pondered the irony as I drank my fill. Here I drank the very water that would kill me in the next few minutes. Despair slid down my throat with every swallow.

After the last gulp, I grabbed the top of the mud wall and struggled to pull myself up. Finally, I balanced on the edge. The cool darkness seemed to invite me in. My heart pounded in fear, and tears made tracks down my cheeks, but soon my suffering would be over. I took a deep breath, and leaned forward.

"What are you doing?"

The rough voice startled me. I nearly lost my grip. A slight man in his thirties, wearing the clothing of a farmer, gazed at me with suspicion.

Jump now, I thought. He cannot reach you in time. But I felt embarrassed to take my life while someone watched. So I lied. "I am waiting for someone."

"You should be at home," he said, narrowing his eyes. "You're coming with me."

I did not know his name, but of course he had heard of me, the cripple. I told him I was fine, but he insisted on accompanying me home. I crawled that distance with a heavy heart, having failed at my goal. No one in my village had even noticed my absence. I would have to try again.

The incident shook me, but I remained determined. A few weeks later, I undertook the journey a second time.

Just entering the clearing made my soul shrivel at the thought of what I would really do this time. My chest began heaving with sobs, and tears fell from my swollen eyes.

Despite the despair that threatened to turn me around, I gripped the mud wall and pulled to the top, balancing on my belly. I stared down into the dark depths, tears dripping into the unknown.

"Boy! Get down from there!"

To my shock, the same thing happened. This time, an old man chanced to walk by.

I hurriedly smeared the tears from my cheeks with the back of my hands, but I know he saw. He could not miss my heaving chest and the tortured expression on my face. He put his hand on my arm to steady me as I slid down.

"Come," he said in a gruff voice. "I will see you home."

With a deep breath, I tried to steady my voice. "It is ok. You can go. I will talk to you another time. Leave me here."

"No. I am going that way already. Come with me." When I refused, he threatened to take me by force. He made sure to follow me on my slow journey home.

Anger burned in my heart. Was God so cruel that he would keep me even from this? From escaping the misery he refused to save me from? I did not permit the thought that perhaps God had another plan in mind.

There had to be another way to take my life than returning to the cursed well. Time passed, and I thought of plan after plan, discarding one after another.

One sultry morning, I dragged myself toward the latrine. Bothersome flies buzzed around my face, alighting on my skin, but my hands were employed for crawling, so I was unable to brush them away. My spirits had sunk so low I could hardly endure the day stretched before me.

On my way back, I slowly passed by the hut where the pesticide was kept. Memories from before the snakebite invaded my mind. Thoughts of carrying water and pesticide for the cattle, and the approving smile on Daddy's face. Then the agonizing remembrance of the burning poison as Daddy poured the concentrated liquid into my wounds.

My body froze, one hand sinking into the cool edge of a mud puddle. That was my solution! If the pesticide was so dangerous to skin, surely drinking it would kill me. I frowned. Irony again. The last time, the pesticide saved my life. This time, the pesticide would end my life. Finally, I would find freedom from worldly pain.

With one excuse or another, I lurked near the hut until no one was around. I slipped inside and made my way to the bedroom. Daddy kept the poison in a hidden place under the bed, closed off so small children could not have access. At age thirteen, I was not a small child anymore, but almost a man. A man who could not endure another day of life. My fingers closed around one of the two-liter bottles. I reached for a small container to use as a cup. I planned to drink it all.

Every sound made me jump, and my heart raced with the threat of discovery. I settled myself at the base of the bed. The place I would die.

With the bottle propped between my crossed legs, my stomach clenched in revulsion at what I intended to do. Sweat dripped down my temples and mixed with my tears as I uncapped the container. The acrid smell made my nose wrinkle. I poured the liquid into the cup and stared into the amber contents.

Take it.

The voice—deep, vibrating, insistent—jolted through me. I felt I must obey.

The thought of swallowing felt like agony. Though six years had passed since the snakebite, just the memory of the excruciating burning of my flesh sent a wave of panic through me. I closed my eyes and recounted the misery of the last several years. Reminded myself of the pain, the hurt feelings, the absence of a future.

With a deep breath, I lifted the cup to my lips. The poison touched my tongue and I jerked it back when the burning started.

If you do this, you will die. If you do this you will DIE!

What was that? My hands began to shake, and I set the cup down. The voice, different from the first, had sounded all around me and inside me at the same time. But gentle. Loving. Impossible.

I lifted the cup once more.

The small voice spoke again. *You need Jesus.* Just as clear as if someone sat beside me—but no one was there. I thought for a long moment about my previous failed attempts. Perhaps killing myself was wrong. Perhaps God had not abandoned me after all.

Go to the church.

Fear consumed my mind and heart, and deep conviction settled within. Now my whole body shuddered, despite the jungle heat.

With shaking fingers, I poured the pesticide back, screwed the cap on the bottle, and slipped out of the hut. But even in that short journey, I knew my heart had changed somehow.

Was I ready?

Friday

OVER THE NEXT days and weeks, that strong, authoritative, yet reassuring voice spoke to me again and again.

You need Jesus.

Sometimes I heard the voice when others were around, but no one looked up or seemed to hear what I heard. Most of the time, the voice spoke when I lay sleepless on my mat, the darkness gathered close. Those were the moments when thoughts of ending my life usually plagued me, and I found comfort that the voice—I was beginning to think of him as my friend—kept me company through the lonely hours.

Had I been wrong? Did God care after all? Perhaps he did not hate me. Perhaps he saw me and knew me. Could I talk to God as a person?

Finally, after three weeks, I made a decision. I would go to the born-again Christian church. Aunt Jane had been attending one. Perhaps the people there could tell me if I really needed Jesus.

I knew I needed *something*—or someone.

From the moment I heard the voice, my thoughts of suicide vanished. No one had helped me as this voice had. In my desperation, I knew I needed to find out more.

When Sunday came, I got up early, cleaned myself well, and changed into my best clothes. Others in the family were preparing to attend the Catholic church. I reached for the comb to fix my hair, but one of my aunts grabbed it first.

"You're not going to church," she said. "We need to get ready."

"But I *am* going to church," I insisted. "I am serious."

But she did not listen to me.

Well, then. I will not go to church, I decided. I crawled away, sulking, and watched each one leave. But even then, I heard the voice.

You need Jesus.

Day or night, no matter what I did, I heard the words. The voice was so frequent, that I became restless. Nothing I did seemed as important as obeying that voice.

Friday morning dawned, and I knew I could not wait for Sunday to arrive again. I must go to church that day.

After preparing myself, I set out at noon. The sun beat down with such intensity as I began the journey.

The church was located about two and a half kilometers from home. The journey was daunting on my knees—even farther than my solo trips to the well. The distance increased as I zig-zagged back and forth across the road to avoid the deep ruts and mud puddles. My knees ached, and my legs bore the testimony of the trip with ragged scratches and deep scrapes. But I kept on, determined to find answers for my life.

However, deep worry gnawed at my soul. I had rejected the Christian religion and shouted angry accusations at God. I had participated in the witch doctor rituals. Was there any hope for me? Could a God so powerful and mighty forgive me—or would he punish me further? Perhaps what people said was true, that I was bound to be a violent person. God may have seen my future and allowed my disability to prevent me from hurting others. My thoughts tormented me as I inched closer to the church.

Finally I arrived and hesitantly made my way up the trail toward the hut that served as the church building. Aunt Jane and two other ladies knelt beside the small mud-walled structure, stacking dried grass to replace worn sections on the thatched roof. They chattered in cheerful voices, sometimes breaking into song as they worked.

I hung back, uncertain of my reception. Would the women see through me and know the bitterness that consumed my heart?

When they noticed me in the shadows of the bushes, they greeted me with warm words.

"Hello Canisius," Aunt Jane said. "You have traveled a long way! It is good to see you."

"Come! Join us!" said a woman with a bright red headscarf. Her eyes twinkled, as if she knew a secret.

Was she amused by the way I crawled? I started to turn away.

"You look thirsty. Here, have a drink."

As the woman brought over a dipper of water, her eyes stayed locked on mine. They didn't travel over my body, and I detected no revulsion or pity. Maybe I would stay a little longer.

A tiny woman, shriveled with advancing years smiled at me. Despite the layers of wrinkles lining her face, her expression looked kind and loving. "We are repairing the roof of the church. But it is not proper for us women to climb up and layer the grass."

Aunt Jane added, "Would you help us?"

Few people asked me for help, beyond the toddlers who clung to my shorts. My family assumed there was little I could do to assist with anything. A crack broke the surface of my bitter heart.

"Yes. I will be glad to help you."

Though my legs were useless for walking, my arms had grown strong from crawling. I found some trees nearby that I could climb to get to the top. Soon I looked down at the women from the roof. I tore off the old, cracked thatch. They passed me thick sections of grass, which I overlapped around the roof until it reached the top. The women told me their names, and I introduced myself.

Mary, the woman with the red scarf, grinned up at me. Her white teeth glowed against her dark skin. "Look at you, Canisius. You are right now building the house of God, serving him even before your decision to be a born-again Christian. It is a prophetic word. You will serve God the rest of your life. You need Jesus in your life."

Her last words, so similar to the voice I had been hearing for three weeks, almost caused me to lose my balance. Could God want me? Could I be useful? Perhaps I had a future after all.

As the women chattered, I learned that they had planned an overnight at the church, as they lived some distance away. They had come to bless their pastor, a man named Isaac, who was leaving to go to a technical school.

At this moment, I was determined to obey the voice I had been hearing. My life was a mess, full of hurt, bitterness, and hatred. I *did* need this Jesus. But how was I to contact him?

Once finished with the roof, I climbed down. I pulled my pouch of tobacco and cigarette papers from my pocket. "Can someone bring me a flame?" Then I made a grave announcement. "I will have my last smoke, and give the rest to you. From now on, I am giving my life to Jesus."

I lit one cigarette after another. The clouds of smoke probably looked like the bush was on fire. Then I handed the my smoking supplies to Mary. At that moment, I knew I was surrendering my heart and life to Jesus. My soul was flooded with relief. I had never in my life experienced anything so deeply real and personal. God was someone I could know.

Pastor Isaac arrived, and the women told him why I was there. He greeted me with love. After hearing my story, he said, "Canisius, you don't have to go through ancestors with the witch doctor, or saints with the priest to talk to God. He longs to have a relationship with you. God sent his son,

Jesus, to pay the penalty for all the wrong you're done—and the wrong I've done. He will forgive you and wipe you clean so that you can talk to him directly.

We knelt down and Pastor Isaac prayed with me. I prayed for God to forgive me of the things I had done wrong—all the bitterness and hatred and despair that had filled my heart. I prayed, believing that Jesus heard my cry for help, and he filled my heart with such assurance of his forgiveness that joy consumed me and lifted my spirit. For a moment, I even forgot that I was the cripple—the boy who brought shame to his family. I knew in an instant that this Jesus was God. The God who saw me—and loved me and was not ashamed to call me his own.

I was somebody to him.

▲▼▲

All this happened on a Friday when I was thirteen years old. I call it my very own Good Friday. The depressed cripple became full of joy. The boy who felt no one cared found love so deep and wide he would never plumb its depths. The hurt and bitter young man found a deep river of peace—and a best friend.

I fell in love with Jesus—the one who had not rejected me but had protected me. For as I began to think through the tragic events of my life, I saw God's hand on me.

Even that day in the jungle after the snake bit me. The rainstorm that I despised caused me to run, and though running spread the venom, the speed surely saved my life.

And when I was poised—twice—at the edge of the well. The thought came to me that so long ago, the witch doctor had once prophesied that one of my father's sons would drown. That was an evil plan for me, one I learned came from God's enemy, the devil. And God prevented his success.

Just as my daddy carried me after the snakebite, and brought me to the hospital on the bicycle and on the tractor, God loved me like a father and saved my life time after time. He even sent his own son to pay for the wrong things I had done. God treasured me, though I had refused to see it. And eventually, I began to realize something.

Nothing can kill you when God has his hand on your life.

Pastor Isaac invited me to stay at the church for the entire weekend, through Monday, and I agreed, for I did not want to miss anything I could learn about Jesus. I sent a message to my village so no one would worry about me.

I began to learn to pray. To serve. To channel my passion for Jesus.

It was as if he whispered, *Through me, Canisius, you will be somebody. Somebody to serve and help others and bring them the same joy and hope I have given you.*

▲▼

My new life centered around church, and the Wednesday, Friday, and Sunday gatherings. No matter what the weather, no matter how muddy the roads, or how exhausted I felt, I made the five-kilometer round trip without fail. The journey did not feel like a hardship, but a joy.

My hunger to learn about God increased. Aunt Jane read the Bible to me at home every day at noon and before bed. I developed a passion for going into the presence of God, spending hours in prayer.

Oftentimes, the congregation went from village to village to tell people about Jesus. I longed to go with them, but my speed would slow them down.

I told the new pastor, Pastor Joram, "I can be faithful to stay here and pray for all of you. That is my contribution."

Since I could not be part of the evangelism team, I searched for another way to help at the church. I offered to clean and do repairs, but they would not hear of it. When they looked at my skinny body, ripped and torn from my frequent trips to church, they probably wanted to protect me. I appreciated their love and care but longed to serve God in some capacity.

So I began to crawl to church early on Sunday mornings, making my way in the misty dawn light. In the dim church, I took the broom and carefully swept the dirt floor of the building. Then I made my way from bench to bench, from mat to mat, laying my hands in each place where one of my new brothers and sisters would sit.

"God, King of Glory, if anyone comes today with a problem, please help them. Provide for them. Protect them. Bring them peace," I prayed.

Here, at last, was something I could do for others. I felt grateful, but I longed to be used for so much more. To be able to share with others the joy and love I had received.

Though my life had been full of pain and heartache, I knew that so many others experienced even worse. Though others might not have a great physical disability, the effects of war, abuse, illness, and so many other things left scars just as debilitating as the things I suffered.

Could God use my suffering to reach others?

Boots

AS TIME WENT on, my hunger to keep learning did not relent. I wanted to know more about Jesus. Though Aunt Jane continued to read the Bible to me, I could not be satisfied with the moments when she was free from her responsibilities. If only I had been able to attend school, to learn to read, I could read the words of God for myself.

The notion of school burrowed inside me like a termite, and would not let me rest. I crawled to church earlier on Wednesdays and Fridays, when we held evening meetings. In the quiet, empty church, I fasted and prayed, pleading with God for an opportunity to attend school. My fourteenth birthday passed, and the idea still seemed impossible. Ugandan children went to school for a total of sixteen years starting at age three or four. How could God accomplish this for me?

However, I learned from the Bible stories Aunt Jane read, that God especially enjoyed doing the impossible. As a teenager, David, who would later become king, went to visit his brothers where they served the army of Israel in war. A great giant and warrior named Goliath hurled insults about God at the Israelite soldiers. He dared the army to choose one man to fight him alone. No one had the courage to face the nine-foot man in battle. Yet little David volunteered.

"Why do you think David did that, Canisius?" Aunt Jane asked me.

"Hmm." I thought hard. Then a smile stretched my cheeks. "I know! Because Goliath was so big, David knew he could not miss the target!"

Aunt Jane chuckled, but I knew that David saw an opportunity. And God was the one who helped David's little stone knock that great big man down. And if God could do that, surely he could help me find a way to attend school. I needed David's mindset to help me with this challenge.

You see, David chose five stones in preparation to meet the giant. He did not know that God would guide the first stone to strike the great man down. He was prepared for God's victory, no matter how many stones he needed. I longed to adopt the same perspective.

I took my request to God. Most seriously, I began to fast and pray, asking God for an opportunity. "Please, God," I prayed. "I long to read your words by myself. It is not enough to hear someone else read them. If I can learn to read, I promise to serve you for the rest of my life." This was not just a childish whim. I meant every word of my promise.

And my God heard me.

▲▼▲

As time went on, I thought about ways to protect my knees. I remembered Daddy's black rubber boots that he always wore in the rainy season. One day, while he took a nap, I crawled into the hut and dragged his boots outside. My heartbeat rattled against my ribs at the thought of Daddy waking up to find I had snatched his boots.

My mind had already been working, thinking about how boots like these might be an answer to my prayers. I had begun to learn that sometimes our challenges become a source of innovation.

Both my legs were small and withered from the effects of the polio. I bent each leg and slid them knee-first into the boots. In this way, my knees went to the bottom of the boot, where the heel normally rested.

Now, when I crawled on my hands and knees, my knees were protected from the ground by the soles of the boots. I quietly returned the boots beside Daddy's bed. Something like this could make such a difference in my life.

When I mentioned the idea to the rest of my family, I could see in their glazed expressions that they didn't understand how useful boots could be for me. As I had no money to buy a pair, I watched always, to see if I could find some.

Now, in post-war Uganda, poverty was universal. To survive those economic times meant to reuse and recycle everything until there was nothing left. So a pile of refuse in Uganda really had no further use at all. If the owner could not make the item work any longer—it was beyond repair. My chances of finding boots seemed small.

Sometimes I crawled to the church when no one was there. I arrived early in the morning, bringing no food or water with me. I knelt in the church and prayed all day long about learning to read—sometimes all night, too. Such was the seriousness of my request.

I believed that Jesus could conquer my illiteracy. And Jesus would do that through the time spent on my knees. My knees served an important role in my transportation, but I was discovering that these hours on my knees in prayer were even more necessary.

As usual, my hands, knees, and legs were a mess, torn and muddied from my three trips back and forth to church each week. I never missed a single service, no matter the weather, the state of the road, or the pain from my ravaged skin. I crawled no matter what.

Sometimes Pastor Joram, planned an all-night prayer service. In order to attend, Aunt Jane and I had to complete all our chores first, which meant we often could not leave home until around midnight. On those occasions, due to the darkness, dear Aunt Jane would carry me the whole way on her back, even in the pouring rain. She blessed me so much with her generosity and taught me how to be there for others in need, serving with joy and happiness. Still, I realized that crawling this way for the rest of my life could not work for me.

For this problem, too, I prayed that God would reveal a solution. And so he did.

One day in 1992, I crawled home as usual. On the way, I passed a cluster of houses. Something black caught my eye in a pile of rubbish, and I moved closer to investigate. Underneath the trash lay a pair of rubber boots.

The rubber boots I found were in a sorry state. Great rips and holes covered both boots, the soles were worn through, and I wondered if there was any use in trying my idea. But I had no money, and here I had at least something to work with. I dragged them home and set to work.

My experience in making knife handles became useful in my endeavor. I heated the blade of a wide knife and held the hot metal to the rips in the boots, melting them together again. For some of the larger holes, I used whatever rubber scraps I could find—yellow, blue, black, and red—and melted them to cover the gap. My boots did not look handsome, but they would serve their purpose.

They reminded me of another Bible story that Aunt Jane read, about a boy my age named Joseph—the same name as my brother. He was not treated well by his family, and he wore a coat of many colors. God sent him to a foreign land, where he showed many people the power of God.

I identified with Joseph. Now I had a pair of boots of many colors. I did not know if God could use me as he had Joseph, but I was willing. Oh, how willing.

I looked kind of funny with my invention. Walking on my knees, my feet were off the ground, up near my bottom. No one had ever seen something like this before. But what a great feeling to be able to move more quickly! My boots not only protected my limbs but helped me keep clean from the mud and puddles along the way. I no longer needed to leave so early to wash off before church, unless we experienced heavy rain. My mobility reached new heights.

When I thought about David and his five stones, I realized that though he had a sling, he picked up his stones along the way. I considered these boots to be my first stone in conquering the giants of mobility and illiteracy. I had only to keep my eyes open for the next stone.

▲▼▲

And so I began to pray for what I saw as my next major obstacle: my legs. Though thankful that my mobility had increased with the boots, the only way I could see myself serving God the way I had promised was if he would heal my legs.

I believed God had power to do just this. I had already seen people healed of many diseases and disorders. And so I prayed.

One day, a man came into the church. I had already knelt there for hours, asking God for healing.

"What do you pray for, Canisius?"

"I am asking God to strengthen my legs so I can walk and serve him with my whole life."

He eased down on the bench nearest me, rubbing a bushy brow with his forefinger. "Well, my son," he said. "If you have been asking God and he has not answered, that means you are lacking in faith."

My jaw dropped open, and I had no answer.

I believed in God's power with every inch of my body. Though I was a recent born-againn Christian, I took God at his word. How could this brother tell me I did not have enough faith? Did not Jesus tell his friends that faith as small as a tiny seed moved mountains?

Confusion fogged my mind, and when it cleared, I found bitterness had rooted and deeply in my heart. This did not seem like something God wanted, but the more I thought about it, during my long treks to and from church, the more I realized something—that more bitterness lay just below the surface.

A single ripple in the water can hide a great hippopotamus. In the same way, my enormous hurt lay within reach. The excitement of my early months as a Christian had distracted me from the negative thoughts I had dwelt on for years. I was surprised they were still there. Somehow I thought choosing Jesus had scoured them away.

I found in my heart the old hurts from the traditional healers and from Lwango. From my siblings, who would not let me touch their books. From my family, who had overlooked me.

"God," I said, "how can I serve you with this bitterness? Release my heart, so I can overcome this."

The journey of forgiveness would not occur in an instant. Like my bicycle ride to the hospital, miles of twists and turns lay ahead.

But the journey had begun.

School

OVER THE NEXT months, God's word became even more real to me. I began to trust God in every area of my life, making God my first priority. And things began to happen. First of all, Daddy suggested that he needed help with his store in Gayaza. Finally, I had a way to be useful! Though I could not keep the cows for my father, surely there was another task I could do, even if I had to crawl. And now I had my boots.

We traveled to Gayaza when I was fourteen years old. Christine lived in that town caring for part of the herd of cows, and Daddy's shop there sold clothes, mattresses, and sewing machines.

"Canisius," Daddy said, "I need someone I can trust to supervise the shop. That way my employees cannot cheat me."

My chest swelled. He considered me capable and trustworthy!

Daddy showed me the shop, and then we went to Christine's house. How wonderful it was to see my dear stepmother. While we were there, my grandmother's sister invited him to the wedding of an uncle. When he told her about me, she said, "Why don't you bring your son?"

Looking back, God planned for Daddy and me to attend that wedding near Nakaseke, Butayunja. For it was there that we learned about a school in the same district. The moment I heard the word 'school', it was all I could think about.

"You should bring him," the man said, taking a swig from his cup. "It is a school begun by two *muzungu*—a white lady and her husband who are missionaries. They are very kind. I think they would take him." And my grandmother's sister lived near to the school.

My heart opened wider than a great banana flower. Could my prayers finally be answered?

My grandmother's sister accompanied us to the school to see if the arrangements could be made. Uganda Gospel Rehabilitation Centre (UGRC) was a boarding school for orphans. Because I was not an orphan, I would continue to live at my grandmother's sister's house. I would have to crawl to and from school, but I did not care. They agreed to let me attend. I felt as if my skin could burst and spill out the great joy that filled me.

My eyes took in the various dormitory and classroom buildings, and the many students in their smart uniforms. Their excited chatter ignited my heart. I could not wait to begin.

The headmaster, David, was also the pastor of the church at the school. I was impressed that he had the same name as King David, who killed Goliath in the Bible.

My grandmother's sister did the talking. "Kindergarten?" she said. "But he is almost fifteen years old, and so much bigger than the others."

Pastor David looked at her kindly. "Canisius has not been to school for so long, and cannot read. He must start at the beginning in order to learn."

I chewed my lip, considering this disappointing turn of events. Kindergarten lasted three years, before seven years of primary school, and six more years of secondary school. At the normal rate, I would not be done with school until the old age of thirty-one!

With all the respect I could muster, I asked, "Would you consider allowing me to begin at primary school? I promise to work very hard, and if I cannot keep up with the work, I will agree to return to kindergarten."

His bushy eyebrows met, as he considered my request. I kept my gaze locked on his. The moment stretched out.

Finally, Pastor David folded his hands. "I see that you are very determined. You may start at primary school in the second grade. But you must devote yourself to your studies."

I nodded vigorously, eyes wide. Crawling was exhausting, and I was accustomed to that hard work. Being allowed to learn was a pleasure. The headmaster did not know about my stubborn streak. He would soon see how much I could apply myself.

And so, my career in Daddy's shop ended only a week after it began—but neither of us minded. Anticipation kept me from sleep the night before school started. I woke early and spent time on my knees, committing my school career to God's care, and thanking him for answering this great request. I had spent two years praying for this day.

On my first real day of school since the polio, I rose early. I dressed in my best clothes that I had carefully washed the day before, slid on my multicolored boots—now even more badly worn. My boots, in their patched and sorry state, caused me a moment's worry, but I reminded myself that returning to school after seven years eclipsed any thought of how I looked. I took a deep breath and made my way down the road.

The journey to school took an hour at my slow pace. But I crawled that tiring distance with such joy and gratitude. I longed to sit again at a desk and learn to make sense of the letters and the sounds that accompanied them. To watch the teacher write on the blackboard. To read the Bible for myself at last.

Finally, the school came into sight. My arms and legs shook with fatigue after my lack of sleep the night before.

When I arrived at the boarding school, all the children were milling outside, heading to class after breakfast. School had already been in session for several weeks. One by one, they began pointing and giggling when they saw me coming. A few cried out in fear. Their voices rose with excitement, and soon hundreds of students crowded the pathways near the road.

"Look at that!" one exclaimed.

The children called out to one another, expressing amazement as I made my way slowly toward them.

One boy elbowed the students around him. "How many legs does he have, do you think?"

A classmate responded. "He might have six legs!"

"It looks like a spider."

I took a deep breath and swallowed hard. With all my longing for school, I had not given thought to how I would be received. This was not the welcome I had hoped for in my new school.

But friendships began, nevertheless. And there were so many things to be involved in. The orphanage church had five choirs. I loved to listen to those beautiful voices blending joyfully in song. I wanted so badly to sing. While my legs did not work, my voice was fine and I found such joy in singing. Praising God satisfied my soul better than food in my belly. My voice, free and unlimited, traveled farther than my frail body ever could.

I watched the choir members. They swayed, stomped, stepped, clapped. They stood tall and straight, proud to belong. Valued. Needed.

But they did not want me. I learned that it is difficult for many others to welcome someone with a disability, even when it is in their power to do so. I tried to hide my disappointment.

But my classes brought me great joy. I was learning at last!

"A, B, C, D..." the class chanted the alphabet in unison under our teacher's instruction.

Though I eagerly participated in everything our class did, I felt a little out of place. My classmates were about six years old. Their high tones along with my deep voice sounded strange and emphasized the fact that I was almost ten years older than my peers.

When the first week ended, Pastor David came to me with a gift. He held a pair of rubber sandals in his hands.

"Canisius, I see that you are crawling to and from school, and it is hard to keep your hands clean. These sandals will protect your hands from the rocks and the mud."

Tears filled my eyes at the generosity of my new pastor. Surely his salary did not allow for extravagances like this. Those sandals meant so much to me, and ensured I spent less time cleaning off after arriving at my destinations. Now I had six shoes to wear: two sandals on my hands, two boots on my knees, and two shoes on my feet. How funny I must have looked!

I made many friends at UGRC, and before long I was finally invited to join one of the choirs. Relationship is a great bridge to overcome the issues of disability. But best of all, I found a close friend. Sebastian and his brother, Joseph, lost their parents in the war. Though Sebastian was younger than me, he had also started school at a later age, so we had much in common. He already knew how to read and write, and he held my arm to help me form my letters as I learned to write. We had such a close connection. Many people thought we were brothers, because we looked similar, and did everything together. Where one went, the other went. Even in our grades, we took turns placing number one and number two. We shared the good and the bad in our lives.

With Sebastian's help, I worked harder than ever, and within three months of starting second grade, I was beginning to read and write, and soon was at the top of my class. What joy filled my heart! While many Bible passages were beyond my comprehension, I could finally understand some of them on my own.

▲▽▲

Almost a month after I started school, I crawled to church for the Sunday service. My multi-colored boots had sprung a new hole, and I told myself to see if I could patch it the next day.

At one point in the service, Pastor David asked me to come to the front.

"Canisius has been such a joy to have in our congregation already. Though he is only fifteen years old, he puts many of us to shame with his attention to his studies, his prayer life, and his willingness to serve wherever God calls." He winked at me, then turned back to the congregation. "Brothers and sisters, I challenge you. With the way this boy gives to God so selflessly, can we not give so that he can continue to serve?" Pastor David continued, "Let us take an offering, and buy a new pair of boots for Canisius. Please, find something that you might give."

I bit my lip, and looked over the crowd of my brothers and sisters, all grinning back at me. These men and women had no more money than my family, and yet one after the other, they came forward to give their donation.

Pastor David took the money to Kampala the next day. When he returned, he carried a bag. Out of the sack, Pastor David pulled a brand new pair of rubber boots! They gleamed black and shiny in the light from the windows. No holes! No rips! No worn soles!

Oh, what an encouragement those boots were. If I could not have the ability to walk, these boots were the next best thing. I slid them on and the next Sunday joined the choir as we sang praise to God for the greatest gift of all—the gift of his own son, Jesus Christ.

▲▼▲

The entire school buzzed with excitement. For weeks, we had heard that the school's founders were coming to visit. I had not experienced this before, but the children were full of anticipation and curiosity. We prayed for Lovie and Syvelle Phillips each day, that they would have a safe trip to our school.

One day, as I made my way up the steps of the school, I saw a beautiful sight. A woman, a *muzungu*, came to greet me. Her skin was white as a cloud, and her hair looked like the color of the tall grass when it turns golden in the dry season, and lay in waves. Her arms stretched out to me, and her smile invited me in. Normally I would be shy to embrace a *muzungu*, but she seemed different.

"My name is Lovie Phillips," she said, bending down to give me a hug. She held me at arms length, and her bright, laughing eyes roamed my face in a way that made me feel like a great treasure. She didn't stare at my legs encased in my boots or seem bothered that she had to bend over so far.

"Pastor David has been telling me about you. Come, and meet my husband."

Lovie introduced me to Pastor Syvelle Phillips. Later I came to discover that they had come from America and began the orphanage school in 1987, just a year after the civil war in Uganda ended. With all the killing that had gone on in my younger years, thousands of children were left orphaned. Lovie and Syvelle often left their home in the United States and came to visit the places of healing and comfort they had provided. Hundreds of orphans benefitted, not only in Uganda but other countries also.

The thought of surviving without Daddy or Mama, even though Mama was far away, made me thankful that I only had a struggle with my mobility. The idea of family members being slaughtered was too much to consider.

Both Lovie and Syvelle became like parents to me. They were not always there, as they traveled between the different ministries they had begun. Every time they visited was always a big day for us students—partly because they brought gifts. It is hard to describe what it meant for us to receive gifts from America. Lovie and Syvelle spoke to our school general assembly and afterward met with each of us. Our hearts were totally won over by their love for us.

Lovie and Syvelle, who I soon began calling Mama Lovie and Papa Syvelle, always had an encouraging word or some wisdom for me to consider. Their love, care, and humility were great examples for me. These helped me keep going when the work was demanding.

What a difference, when someone believes in you.

Prayer

BESIDES LEARNING AT school, one of my greatest joys was prayer. That may sound strange to some people, but I had a passion for spending time with the God who had loved me and saw potential in me. The same God who saved me from harming myself, who made me feel useful and treasured. Praying for others gave me the sense that I was making a great difference in the lives of people. And just like spending time getting to know a friend, through prayer I began to know my God through a close relationship. At the orphanage school, my classmates groaned when it was my turn to say the blessing because my prayers were so long. Prayer was a big part of every day, alongside school—and crawling.

My school days soon took on a regular routine. In the mornings, I dressed for school. I did not yet have money to purchase a uniform, and I longed to dress smartly like the other students, but I knew I must be patient.

If I had books or homework to bring along, I slid them inside my shirt and tucked the tail of my shirt in my shorts to keep them contained. Some days were exasperating, because the books were heavy enough to make my shirt come out, and they fell to the ground. It upset me most when the ground was muddy, and my books became dirtied. I never liked this situation, but I had to bear it, so I pressed on.

Looking clean and smart was important to me, but the weather seemed like my adversary. When I reached school every day, my first stop was the well, where I washed myself before I went to class. In the rainy season, I arrived at school wet and smeared with mud, which sometimes required a change of clothes. During the dry season, mud was not such an issue, but the wind caused me to be covered with dust, making me cough and sneeze.

After crawling to school, which took an hour, the school day ran until 3:00. Then I made my way home to change clothes. Now it was 4:00. Once I changed into more casual clothes, I made the trip back to school. Why? I was determined to devote a portion of my day to prayer, and I wanted to pray at Pastor David's church, right next to the school. I had begun to attend there when I started school. I arrived at the church at 5:00 pm and spent the next three hours of every weekday on my knees in prayer. At 8:00, I started the journey home, and at nine in the evening I began to work on my homework. I stayed focused on schoolwork until it was completed, and I was certain that I understood what the teacher had taught. Then, bleary-eyed, I fell into my bed.

Each morning I awakened early, as I wanted to begin the day with fasting and prayer, and seek God about my future. I rose at two in the morning, and crawled back to the church, where I prayed for several hours until five, when the time came to leave once more for school.

I found that when we seek God, he answers us. God spoke to me in these times of prayer. A vision came to my mind. In the vision, I spoke before a large group of people.

"God, is this vision from you? I can hardly believe it possible that someone would listen to me in the condition I find myself."

God made it clear that serving him—what we called ministry—was part of his plan for me. But I still held back. Who could listen to me talk about God's power, when God had not healed my legs? I remembered how hard it was to believe that the traditional healer, Mulego, could heal my legs when he could not walk himself. Already, other believers questioned my faith in God's ability to heal. If I had not received healing myself, who could believe my words?

"I know you have good plans, God. I long to serve you. I promised when I first believed that I would give you the rest of my life. Would you let me be able to walk? I know you have the power to strengthen my legs, but how will your plan come to pass?"

▲▼▲

One day when we had a school break, I took myself to the church, determined to stay there until God helped me walk so that I could truly serve him. First, I closed all the doors and windows of the church, blocking out the sounds of people, birds, and weather, so that I would not be disturbed. I laid my hands on my legs, bent them and stretched them as I prayed. I believed with every fiber of my soul that God had enough power in his little finger to heal me many times over.

I stayed there for six days, taking no food or water. I cried. I prayed. I begged.

"God," I said, hoarse from dehydration. "First perform a miracle. If you raise me up, then I can do what you have for me." I shifted position on my aching knees. "I have seen the lame walk. I have witnessed the sick healed. Nothing is too hard for you."

And God spoke in the quiet of the still church.

My son, Canisius. You ask for healing of your legs—such a little thing. But I have already healed you from the greatest and most crippling condition—the condition of your soul. Without forgiveness of your wrongdoing that kept you from relationship with me, you would face eternity apart from me.

I am keeping you the way you are so that people will see I am not a respecter of persons. Go and preach. Though you must drag yourself through the dark and mud, I have a plan for your life. I have a plan for you to bless those who hurt in ways far worse than what you have experienced.

I bowed my forehead to the floor, gratitude filling my heart. "Oh God, let your will be done. If this is the way, I am willing."

Pastor David happened to come by on the sixth day I was there. "What are you doing, Canisius? You look terrible. Your eyes are sunken, and you can barely sit up."

I explained my mission to tender-hearted Pastor David. He understood, being a great intercessor himself.

"Oh, Canisius. You need to take something. Here," he said, finding a jug. "Take some water. You are hurting your body."

Pastor David watched me gulp the water down. He studied me with his warm brown eyes. "My son, when you seek God with your heart, honestly, God speaks. He has revealed to me that you are going to nations. You will speak to thousands."

God confirmed my vision with his words. But in my heart I thought, "But I can only read simple sentences!" It seemed too hard to believe.

Still, God echoed back. *You need to go.*

Other church members also confirmed what God had spoken to my heart with prophecies God revealed to them. After this, I began to trust God even more. My hope was rejuvenated. I believed anything was possible. God had made me someone. Someone of value. But even more important, *God* was the someone, far more than me.

Potential

MY FAITH STRENGTHENED. I turned my focus from my disability to God's ability. His plan for me meant that I needed to go beyond my disability. I did not doubt that God might choose to heal me someday, but I decided to trust his strength and timing to do it. I would glorify him if he did heal my legs, but I would not let my mobility stop me from what God was calling me to accomplish.

Pastor David was such an encouragement in my life. He loved me so much, I could feel it. He was a great example of a servant leader. He saw potential in me and challenged me.

One day, he said, "Canisius, I believe God wants you to become a preacher. What do you think?"

The idea of going before the congregation and preaching a sermon sounded overwhelming. Yet God had said to preach. Pastor David taught me, trained me, prayed with me, and practiced with me.

My first turn to preach was accompanied by a bad case of nerves. I did little more than read the Bible verses out loud. I crawled away from the front of the church, discouragement weighing every movement.

Pastor David met me outside the church. "Wow, Canisius! What kind of a preacher you will be! I see great potential in you."

My dear pastor's vision for me helped me move forward. I learned the value of encouraging words. Sometimes Pastor David had to travel, and he often left all the church activities in my hands. I learned how to manage my time better.

So on the weekends, I did not rest. I had committed to serve God with my whole life. Why not start now? So many years were lost during my illnesses and recovery, so much time spent in sadness, that I felt eager to give back to my God who loved me and granted me new life. A purpose. I could finally be somebody—but not for selfish reasons. To help others know the peace and love I experienced.

Before long, I began to receive invitations from local churches to come and speak to them. While I did not share the story of how I came to be crippled, I simply shared how

Jesus set me free from all the wrongs I had done on that special day I still call 'my Good Friday', and how he changed my life. And people responded to God's message. They repented. They found peace. They found freedom.

My joy and happiness increased with each opportunity to minister. Whether the church was one or two kilometers away, I felt better after I served, even if my arms and legs shook with exhaustion when I reached home. If I couldn't go to a speaking engagement, I felt out of sorts and restless.

Preaching while in primary school. Syvelle Phillips is standing on the right.

Some ministry was in villages, and sometimes we gathered churches together for revival. People were healed, filled with the Holy Spirit, and many were encouraged in their faith. Demons were cast out, and incredible miracles happened. God's power was at work—even through a crippled boy like me. From that time, I knew God could use me if I just said yes.

Soon, even though I was still just a fifteen-year-old boy, more invitations arrived. As I spent my Saturdays and Sundays crawling to and from the various speaking engagements, I noticed something unusual. Many youth attended the churches, but these teenagers looked and acted no different from the youth who did not have a relationship with Jesus. What was wrong? Why were they not using their youthful energy to serve and share about Jesus?

The churches were not unified in any way, so I spoke with the leaders of the various congregations in the district, and proposed a youth ministry to train and mentor young people to serve. To win the youth, we needed unity. The church leaders liked my idea and asked me to lead this endeavor. We called it Luwero Joint Youth Christian Forum. Though the planning and meetings took much time, I enjoyed serving in this way, even though I found I needed to stay up later to complete my primary school studies. Together, the other leaders and I planned events, conferences, ministry opportunities, networks of prayer, and training sessions. The group eventually grew to more than two thousand youth.

▲▼▲

I learned a great lesson during this time of fledgling ministry. Sometimes, we can share even a negative event in our life and God can use it to encourage someone.

While I was still at the orphanage I needed a new pair of trousers. Daddy had given me a little money, so I crawled to the market and found a pair. They were the most expensive item of clothing I had ever bought—20,000 Ugandan shillings—but they were of good quality and would last for some time—especially protected by my new boots. However, the trousers were too big for me, especially with my short, skinny legs. A tailor lived some miles away, and I made the journey to take my trousers for adjustment. He promised to cut off the extra length and sew the hem.

The miles back to class passed quickly because I was filled with so much happiness. "This is very good," I thought. "I will have nice-looking trousers to wear when I preach in the churches." I couldn't help but think that I had come a long way from a boy with holes in his shorts.

Excitement filled me when I traveled again to pick up my trousers. When I reached his home, the man held up my pants. Instead of trimming them to my height, he had made them into shorts!

Disappointment filled my heart. "God, why did this happen?" I complained. "Why did you allow this money to be wasted?"

That evening, during my prayer time at the church, I felt so restless and angry about those shorts. The situation became magnified in my mind until it felt like a huge issue. I prayed about the shorts, and I probably complained some more to God. But as I did, something surprising happened. God sent some questions to my heart.

Canisius, do you not know that there are some people who lose family members to death, and yet still continue on? Are there not people who lose property far more valuable than these mere trousers, yet they don't give up and complain?

Conviction filled my heart. I had magnified my insignificant situation until it seemed insurmountable. Likewise, I remembered how David's brothers, in the shadow of the giant, could only see Goliath's size. They were so overwhelmed and lost their courage, so they ran the other way.

"God," I prayed. "Help me to keep from magnifying my problems to the point that I see them as larger than you. Help me to know that you are always larger than the problem. I will let go of the trousers. They are unimportant in the perspective of your plan for me." And so, I left the issue, feeling freedom from the weight of anger and bitterness.

Sometime later, I preached at a local church, and something reminded me of the trouble with my trousers. I shared my testimony about that incident. One lady in the congregation with a colorful dress and headscarf came to me afterward and told her story.

"I had gone to the hair salon and asked the woman to do my hair. She did a terrible job, and I was very angry. I lost 5000 Uganda shillings." She tucked in the scarf that hid the hair she was so ashamed of. "I was bitter and angry with this woman. I didn't know if I was going to forgive what she did. But then you shared how you lost 20,000 Uganda shillings—several times what I lost—and forgave anyway. I realized my need to forgive this woman. Now I feel so relieved and happy, like a weight has been lifted off of me."

She gave me a hug and moved on. I thought about this on my way home. Sometimes we don't know what we might go through, and that someone else is also going through a similar thing. And if we share our life experiences, even the negative ones, they can help another person to handle or overcome those issues. Each of us experience failures and heartaches, achievements and joys. We all have a story to tell that might be just the thing to encourage someone else.

▲▼▲

In August of 1993, wonderful news came to us via radio. The announcer said, "After three years of conflict between the Rwandan Hutu-led government and the Rwandan Patriotic Front, a ceasefire agreement was signed."

We rejoiced that our family members in Rwanda could experience a more stable environment. Though problems still existed, all of us breathed a sigh of relief. My far away sister, Catrine, was safe, for now.

And then in December, I received yet another gift. Pastor David came with a message for me. "Lovie and Syvelle Phillips have found a donor. Someone in the US offered to sponsor you. You can move into the orphanage!"

I felt overwhelmed with gratitude. No more crawling for an hour each way between school and home and church as I had for nearly a year. This would give me more time to study and pray and serve—and even sleep. This was such a blessing and encouragement. I started 1994 with new resolve, new hope, and increased faith.

I would need all of that in the horrific year to come.

Genocide

ONE HUNDRED DAYS. So much can happen in such a short time.

What can I say about the year 1994? It was the year that changed everything in my world. So much horror, so much death, so much suffering. People in other countries might have thought that another conflict in Africa was a normal thing. But for those of us with family in Rwanda, life was anything but normal.

That spring, I was still fifteen years old, and beginning my second year of school. Moving into the dormitory at the orphanage was such a blessing—mostly. I wore my brand new boots and did not have to travel long distances, at least for my education. But there were some challenges I had to overcome.

I missed my family and looked forward to the school breaks. I had often thought of my sister, Catrine, and wondered how much she had grown during these last five years. How strange to think that she was now ten years old. My thoughts wandered to how she was doing, and if she was happy. She is likely years beyond me in school, I thought wryly.

That year, as the rainy season began, I focused even more seriously on my studies. Though I had started to read, I realized that understanding basic words was not enough. In order to prepare for whatever way God chose to use me, I needed to take advantage of all the education I could obtain. To have any chance of finishing my schooling before age thirty, a great deal of hard work was required.

We received information about the world via radio, and that April, terrible news was broadcast. On April 6th, an airplane carrying both Rwandan president Juvenal Habyarimana and Burundian president Cyprien Ntaryamira was shot down as it descended into Kigali, the capital of Rwanda, killing everyone aboard. Only the year before, Habyarimana had signed a ceasefire with the Rwandan Patriotic Front (RPF). Though the Rwandan president's decision displeased many Hutu citizens, the action brought some level of peace—for a time.

We all wondered: what would happen now? The RPF would certainly be blamed, and hostilities might easily begin again. Naturally, I thought of Catrine. "God, protect her," I prayed. "She is so young."

Our worst fears were realized. The day after the assassination, soldiers, police, and militia executed important Tutsi and moderate Hutu leaders. The authorities set up checkpoints and roadblocks, using each person's Rwandan national identity card, listing their tribe, to identify and kill the Tutsi they found. Houses had been marked in advance with the tribe and number of people living there, to make escape more harrowing.

My appetite fled, as I worried about what might be happening to my aunt, her family, and my dear Catrine. News—accurate news—was not always easy to obtain, as we had only two radio stations. One, controlled by the government, never shared direct news of the slaughter going on. Sometimes the report said, "we are doing a work in such and such an area", which only told us where the worst conflict might be happening, but without specific information. The other, was the international station Voice of America, which gave more details.

Chilling details.

Soldiers, police, and militia had been trained in the art of killing with the machete. They had practiced on huge herds of goats so that their methods were both brutal and effective. The government provided lists of names and addresses so that no one could hide, and escape was almost impossible.

Hutus in Rwanda were pressured to participate in the killing. Propaganda on the radio convinced them that Tutsis were dangerous, and must be killed. They were told that Tutsis were like snakes and cockroaches. "You have to kill the snake before it bites! You must spray the cockroaches before they destroy your house!" the radio voices ordered. Neighbor turned against neighbor. No longer solely perpetrated by soldiers and police, now a significant portion of the population became killers as well, wielding machetes, clubs, or any sharp objects to kill and maim in horrific ways.

And then the rapes.

The use of war rape in the Rwandan genocide against the Tutsi was beyond the scope of the imagination. What had come over my countrymen? How could anyone inflict this kind of shame and injustice on the citizens of their own nation, with whom they had lived in peace as neighbors for so many years? We listened via radio with mouths hanging open in shock.

Could the reports really be true?

Sadly, the news was accurate. Soldiers, and some Tutsi who fled the conflict and took refuge in Uganda, confirmed that the reports were not only true but left out many of the most horrific details.

The world seemed to close their eyes to the genocide. The United Nations removed their peace-keeping soldiers, and world leaders chose not to act.

My body felt weak with worry. Prayers for Catrine and Aunt Nzamugura's family, along with Aunt Prisca and my mother's relatives were always on my lips. Focusing on my studies became harder. I lost count of the hours spent on my knees, pleading for the lives of my family and my countrymen, and agonizing over the choices made by the antagonists.

Our church conducted frequent prayer meetings to bring the conflict before the One who longed to love each person. We prayed for the nation as a whole, that peace and healing would begin. And we prayed for our family members, from whom we heard no word. Many members had Rwandan relatives. We had such concern and burden for each of them.

As the weeks dragged on, the numbers of reported dead reached unbelievable proportions. The radio announcers cautioned Ugandans to refrain from fishing or consuming fish caught in Lake Victoria, which borders Uganda to the southeast.

The reason was hard to believe. Thousands upon thousands were slaughtered as they ran, with many trying to hide in the swamps. The killers tossed bodies and body parts by the truckload in the Nyabarongo River, which feeds into the Kagera River. The victims eventually floated down to Lake Victoria. An estimated 11,000 bodies were found in Lake Victoria alone. The stories of what those bodies looked like as they arrived in the lake turned our stomachs.

Ugandans avoided fish, one of the staples, and reports came that the water of the lake smelled very bad.

To make matters worse, some of the Ugandan orphans at school made fun of me because they knew I was Tutsi. "Go back to your country," they teased. "Your people are the reason we cannot eat fish. Maybe it is your family who is making the lake stink."

But those dark thoughts had already consumed my mind. All I could think about was that some of those people floating in the lake could easily be my sweet Catrine and other members of my family. I cried for her, feeling sure I would never see her again. Who could survive against these fierce enemies?

One brief bright spot shone during that terrible time. Pastor David had been trying to connect with World Vision to get some kind of crutches for me. My dad brought me to a hospital to see if they could help. We remained at the hospital for three weeks as the doctors determined if a certain surgery would strengthen my legs. While we waited at the hospital, I watched many people in various conditions who had undergone surgery. They limped or sat hour upon hour.

Watching these people scared me, as I thought they often looked worse than before their surgery. Finally, the doctors gave the verdict. Surgery was not possible for me— the bones of my legs had been too weakened by the polio. They recommended a wheelchair.

Now that my dad had an official recommendation, he was able to purchase a cheap wheelchair. He paid 40,000 Ugandan shillings, which was a good value. The wheelchair was made locally with some thin water pipes, a wooden seat, and rubber wheels.

That wheelchair filled me with such joy! Ever since I had seen the three-wheeled bicycles, I had longed for some way to transport myself.

I felt so proud to return to school with my wheelchair and my heart was filled with gratitude to my dad and to my God. Everyone ran to see what it looked like and begged for a ride. My hopes for the future soared. My rubber boots were finally set aside. Nothing could stop me now.

Well, that was not quite true. Some of my classrooms had steps in order to get inside. The terrain was not easy for the wheels of the chair. I found I needed to keep my boots with me for the times when the wheelchair would not work.

And whenever I had to leave my wheelchair to climb the steps to class, other students always found it. To them, it was not a necessity, but a toy. They took joyrides, and pushed one another very fast down the road, sometimes falling down. I often returned to my chair to find parts of it scratched, dented, or broken. Anger boiled in my heart.

One day, as clouds gathered for a heavy afternoon downpour, the worst happened. Some students played with my chair again, and this time it broke beyond repair. My heart felt just as damaged—shattered even. How could these friends of mine treat my longed-for wheelchair this way? My resentment grew, along with my discouragement.

I had only used that wheelchair for three short months, and there was no money to buy another. My spirits sank as low as the ruts I crawled around as I returned permanently to my rubber boots.

▲▼▲

As the genocide continued, weeks turned into months, and it became even more heartbreaking to listen to the radio.

To hear the details of the atrocities. To continue to wonder about our loved ones.

Finally, about the time of my sixteenth birthday in mid-July, the genocide came to an end when the RPF was able to take over the city of Kigali. The terror had lasted for one hundred eternal days.

How could people so intensely harmed ever live in peace again with their neighbors? Could a country so decimated by war and murder ever recover?

At night, I tossed and turned, visions of Catrine and my relatives driving me to my knees again and again in prayer. Our church discussed how Christians could step in to help.

I learned later that year that Pastor Isaac, who had prayed with me when I became a Christian, moved to Rwanda to minister to the remaining population. I remember thinking that it was a blessing for him to have such a clear call on his life. Pastor Isaac's dad sometimes gave us reports about what he was doing. However, despite all this, I had no desire to go to Rwanda myself. Certainly God had other plans for me.

▲▼▲

One thing that still burdened me—and intensified during this time—was my bitterness and unforgiveness towards others. My long list included the traditional healers, the thoughtless students at school, and even my family for the way I had been treated. And now, I had added the soldiers and killers who may have already slaughtered my little sister, along with an untold number of others.

All I could think about was myself.

One day as I read from the book of Matthew, I came to a story that stopped me cold.

Jesus told of a servant who had been forgiven a great amount of money by the king. He was thankful for the mercy he received, yet went to another man who owed him a small sum and demanded repayment. The debtor begged for mercy, but the servant threw him in jail. When the king heard of the man's behavior, he confronted the servant and sent him to be tortured in prison.

Jesus said, "This is how my heavenly Father will treat each of you unless you forgive your brother or sister from your heart."

Grief struck me, as I considered how I had harbored bitterness and anger in my heart, nursing my negative emotions. In the same way that the snake's venom had spread poison and decay through my physical body, my bitter feelings had done the same with my spirit.

"God," I cried, "how can I serve you with this bitterness? Release my heart so I can overcome this. Help me to move beyond thinking of myself."

I begged God's forgiveness and made the difficult choice to let go of the hurt from those painful situations. I felt as though I had been carrying a heavy pot of water on my head and finally laid it down. The freedom only made me realize that the prison I had remained in was one of my own making. I named each person I needed to forgive, including both traditional healers--and the unkind daughter, Lwango.

I remembered so clearly how I questioned Lwango's cruelty to me when I had done nothing to her. The situation felt like a great injustice. On an even greater scale, the tribal conflict in Rwanda was not so different. I began to understand in a small way, the injustice the Hutu might have felt when they thought they were oppressed by the Tutsi-controlled government in past years. And now the Tutsi felt the same way, as the Hutu retaliated against them.

But even the bitterness and hatred in my heart had caused harm to Lwango. I needed to forgive her in order to be forgiven. I had to let it go.

I began to realize that forgiveness is a choice I make. Forgiveness is not dependent on how much you are hurt. Clinging to the bitterness only hurt me, causing pain and sadness. Once I truly released my bitterness, I felt such comfort, healing, and freedom. I felt my prayers were not hindered; there were no walls enclosing me anymore.

No, it was not easy. I took that hurt. I did not look for retaliation. I took that hurt and let the offender go free. And at the same time, I freed myself.

When I told God years ago that I would serve him for the rest of my life, he took me seriously. I did not know it, but God's plan had been set in motion long ago. God put me in the path of the snake for a reason. He had allowed the measles and especially the devastating polio to bring me to the place he needed me to be in my heart, for the work he had in mind for me.

The lesson of forgiveness stayed with me, for there were many times to come where I had to make the choice to forgive. And years later, in Rwanda, God would use this lesson in an even greater way.

For my bitterness and unforgiveness limited me far more than my lack of mobility. Only when I forgave did I truly become unlimited.

Resurrection

THE YEAR 1995 was a year filled with school, ministry, and continued wonder about Catrine's well-being. The report of the total numbers of people killed in the genocide was one million—and some said that could be a low number. It was impossible to imagine a ten-year-old girl could have survived.

God continued to confirm my call to ministry, but I had no idea of the timing or the location. He had answered so many prayers for me, in regard to mobility with the boots, going to school, and delivering me from bitterness and unforgiveness. There was nothing he could not do. And so, I started praying for another big thing: a wife. The idea seemed impossible—but I began praying for a godly wife, for children, and even for my potential grandchildren. If God had done so many amazing things already, why not ask him for a partner in ministry? I knew that God heard me and would answer my prayers, but I didn't know how it might come about.

During this year, Pastor David asked me to become the leader of the main church choir and a church coordinator, leading all ministries in the pastors' absence. What joy it was to lead the church in worship through music! Long gone were the days when I could only wish to be a part of the choir. God was so good.

On my school breaks, sometimes a family member rode a bicycle to bring me home for a visit. With school about one hundred miles from our village, this was a long way to ride! Usually, my brother Joseph or one of my cousins performed this task—a journey of an entire day to come to my school, and another day to ride me back to the village. And then they repeated the trip when the time came for me to return to school.

I sensed a change in how my family felt towards me. They were happy for me to be learning at school and saw that things were different in my life. They began to see I had a future. I was bold to tell them about Jesus and how he had done so much for my heart, freeing me from my wrongdoing and especially releasing the burden of unforgiveness. I was so grateful for their change in attitude, and my chest swelled with joy each time Joseph smiled and said "let's ride" as we headed back to school on the bicycle.

When we encountered steep hills. Joseph cheerfully got off the bike and pushed it while I rode on the seat.

▲▼▲

On one visit home in 1996, Daddy announced that he had made a decision.

"I am journeying to Rwanda to see what has happened to our family," he said, his expression grave. New wrinkles lined his face that had not been there before the genocide. "Perhaps I can find some of them if they survived."

"And Catrine?" I asked.

"Yes, I will look for Catrine."

And so Daddy left.

It worried us to watch him go, despite the fact that there was more stability in Rwanda. Would we ever see him again? My mind returned to the days when he was kidnapped by the Ugandan soldiers. Things were different now. Back then, I watched Maria throw ashes and scream curses. This time, some of my family members joined me in praying for Daddy's safety and that God would guide him where he needed to search.

Joseph pedaled me back to school, and still I prayed.

One cloudy afternoon, Pastor David came to see me. "I have a message for you from home, Canisius."

I grabbed his hand. My breath stopped as I waited for him to speak.

"Catrine is found! Your father brought her home. She's alive!"

A huge gasp started my lungs again. I wished I could jump up and down like I had as a boy. But I was eighteen now, and even if I could have jumped, I must act like a man.

Pastor David hugged me. "I'm so glad we have a school break coming soon. You'll be able to see her."

I wiped tears from my eyes. "What else did they say?"

He smiled. "When they saw her, it was like a resurrection."

"I can't believe she's alive!"

I spent hours on my knees praising God for preserving Catrine's life. But not all the news was happy. My aunt and uncle, who had been caring for Catrine, did not survive, along with four of their children. Members of Prisca's family died, including her father. Many of my mother's family were killed. The list of dead or missing weighed on my heart. Daddy brought some of my aunt's remaining children back with him.

The days could not pass fast enough until our school break arrived. And the bicycle journey home felt endless.

When we finally arrived in the village, the whole family surrounded us when they came to greet us. My eyes roamed from face to face, searching for Catrine's smile. I had not seen her since she was five, and now she would be a young lady of thirteen, but I felt sure I would recognize her.

"Where is Catrine?" I asked, still balanced on the bicycle.

My stepmother Christine spoke up. "Here she is," she said, with her arm around a beautiful girl.

My eyes searched her face, drinking in the sight of her.

Catrine's gaze slipped past me, and the jolly smile I remembered was not there.

Something prevented me from throwing my arms around her. "Hello, Catrine," I whispered. "It is me, Canisius. I have come home from school."

Catrine looked at me but did not speak. After a short while, she disappeared into Christine's hut.

Christine spoke quietly. "Catrine has seen terrible things. She is not the happy child we once knew. She likes to be alone too much." She pointed toward her hut. "You have endured much pain in your life. Perhaps you can reach her."

I climbed down from the bicycle, slid my black rubber boots on my legs, and crawled to the hut. The interior was dark and cool and smelled of fresh milk. The main room lay empty. I made my way into one of the bedrooms. At first I thought this room was vacant too, but then I saw a slight form on the bed. The blanket was pulled tightly over her head, and she was wrapped up like a cocoon.

"Catrine. I have prayed for you so much. It is good to see you."

No answer. I reached out a hand and softly touched her shoulder. Her body jerked violently and she scrambled to the far side of the bed. In the weak light from the small window, her eyes looked almost like someone dead. She would not meet my gaze.

I understood what Christine said. The lively little sister who left years ago was gone. A haunted girl replaced her.

The family was not sure how to treat Catrine. She participated in family activities but was obviously depressed, and likely traumatized by what she had endured. She did not want to talk about the genocide. Sometimes her attitude shifted dramatically, from forced cheerfulness to sullenness, so most family members just let her be.

I longed for my sister and prayed mightily for God to heal her. But what could I do? She did not want to be touched and did not want to communicate. "God," I prayed, "help me to understand what Catrine needs right now."

For the rest of my school break, I spent most of my time with Catrine. I just sat near her. Sometimes we sat in silence and sometimes I just spoke quietly with her and treated her as tenderly as possible.

I watched her and began to learn her expressions, identifying when she was having a good or bad day, so I could respond as she needed.

When I returned to school, there had been no change. But I reminded myself that whatever she had been through had hurt her very deeply. I needed to be patient and wait for her to be ready to open up to life again.

Each time I rode home for another school break, I prayed during the whole journey. And then, in the village, I sat with Catrine. I told her how I found my rubber boots, for the last time she had seen me I was only beginning to crawl. I shared how the students thought I was a spider on my first day of school. Once in a while, I told her how I met Jesus, and how he healed the broken places in my life.

Little by little, Catrine made progress. A bit of eye contact. A small smile. Touching my hand. Eventually, she began to talk about Rwanda, but only when the two of us were alone.

With all the stories and news reports I had heard, I thought I was ready to hear Catrine's story. But I was not. And Catrine likely has never told me everything. Some wounds are too deep to find words. Some sights too shocking to speak aloud. Some memories too traumatizing to ever mention. I don't know how many people Catrine saw die. I don't know how many bodies she saw on her journey. How many acts of violence she had witnessed. I only know that the light from her eyes seemed extinguished, like a spark from a fire as it rises into the air.

Could that light ever return?

▲▼▲

When the genocide began, Aunt Nzamugura and her husband had nine children, plus Catrine. The day after the president's plane was shot down, the killing started. For ten-year-old Catrine, it began at their neighbor's house.

"I heard screaming and crying for help at the house next door," she said. "Some of our Hutu neighbors slaughtered that entire family."

My uncle was killed soon after. Terrified, Aunt Nzamugura, who Catrine called 'Mama' after so many years there, whispered to the children, "We must run and hide in the banana and sorghum plantations. Let us go to the plantation of our neighbors, the Ndabarinzi family. I know they are Hutu, but they have always been so good to us, such close friends. Besides, their name means 'I am protecting you'."

They ran without bringing anything. Even a small delay could mean death. The neighbors welcomed them. "We must divide you into small groups so that we can hide you more easily."

Aunt Nzamugura told Catrine and her sister-cousins to go in one direction while she and the boys went to a different hiding place. Catrine and her oldest and youngest girl cousins huddled together in that tight space. Through a crack in the cabinet door, Catrine saw different groups meeting with their neighbors and whispering. Fear entangled her heart. *This is our last day. We will not survive.* But she did not want to frighten her cousins even more. They grasped one another's hands in horrified silence.

All too soon, the cabinet door opened. "Come with us," the neighbors said. They took Catrine's two cousins, but not Catrine. She saw the neighbors pulling them toward the banana trees, and watched until they were hidden from sight.

Moments later, agonized screams came from the place they had gone. Screams Catrine recognized immediately. Her body began to shake. "I heard my sisters crying and calling for help. And then the cries stopped. I knew they were killed. And my turn was next."

People were running back and forth everywhere. Most held machetes or sharp sticks, and she didn't want to think about what they would do to her when they remembered she was there. Had Mama and the boys been killed already?

Since everyone seemed busy, Catrine slipped out, trying to act as if she were going to visit the latrine. As soon as she was out of sight of the neighbor's house, she started running toward home. Many people fled in all directions. When she glanced behind her, the killers were following her. Hunting her.

How can this be? she thought. *These people were dear friends and neighbors just yesterday.*

Catrine sped up, scanning for her dear mama. In the chaos, she met another woman, a friend who was the same age as Aunt Nzamugura. Before Catrine could even say a word to this woman, the killers were upon her, hacking at her with machetes, then turning to the next person within reach.

"I managed to slip away again, but I didn't know where to run this time. My home was not safe. Our friends were not safe. So I just followed others—strangers to me— who were running, hoping to get away from this madness. Surely, once outside the town, things would be better."

But she was wrong. No matter where they ran, the neighbors hunted them. The soldiers scoured the bushes for them. The militias chased them.

Catrine saw women—young and old—raped repeatedly. Afterward, their attackers often pierced them with sharp stakes, spears, and knives in places difficult to mention, the points of the stakes exiting through their mouths. For pregnant women, the killers cut their wombs and tore the babies from them while the mothers screamed in agony.

The frightened little group she joined hoped to make their way to the neighboring country of Burundi, where they thought they could find refuge. But in between lay many dangers, not the least of which were the soldiers, police, and Interahamwe militias who longed to rape, torment, and kill.

The soldiers were not the only enemies. The refugees spent so many nights and days without food and water. Some people fainted on the way or fell into deep ditches in the dark and the rain. Others died of hunger. They were so desperate they drank from stagnant puddles of water on the road, causing disease and dysentery. Those that weakened or lagged behind felt the wrath of the killers. Some people paid money to buy a single bullet so that they could end their lives quickly.

"I felt so lost and alone. All my family were probably dead already, and I had no idea where to go or what to do next. A woman in our group by the name of Mpore had been very kind to me, and I stayed near her. At one point, the killers discovered us, and we scrambled to hide in a swampy area full of papyrus. We tried to be so quiet, as we stepped from one clump of grass to another, sometimes having to wade through the swamp water covered with floating papyrus. Mpore was just one step ahead of me when she suddenly disappeared. The swamp just swallowed her up. I never saw her again."

Seeing what happened, the group changed direction, as the killers were still in pursuit. Weeping, Catrine kept looking back, hoping that Mpore would surface in another place. But Mpore was gone.

In their group, those who were heavier did not survive that swamp. Catrine felt that soon she would be all alone, at the mercy of the soldiers.

The journey felt endless. At last, when the border of Burundi finally came in sight, the harrowing times did not end. The Akagera River separated Rwanda from Burundi. Due to the rainy season, the river was at flood stage, the water roiling and deep. There was no bridge in this place, but some people with canoes were helping refugees across.

Others were rigging a rope so people could balance above the strong current. Catrine and her group waited for one of the small boats to return.

More and more refugees gathered on the bank of the river, all of them desperate to make it across. One canoe finally reached the shore, and everyone tried to get into the boat—more than it could hold.

"Suddenly, I heard my name," she said.

"Catrine! Over here!"

When she squinted at the boat, she saw a neighbor, a relative of our uncle. "Come Catrine! Come in the boat!"

The militias were very close, and anyone left on the bank could be killed before another boat returned. She tried to move forward, but everyone was pushing, panicking that they might die so close to freedom. Being only ten, she slipped in between bodies and came within reach of the overloaded canoe. More people jumped on.

"Hurry Catrine! We will care for you!"

Just as she reached for her neighbor's hand, the sailor started the canoe, and it slipped from the bank. Behind, she heard the shouts of the killers. And before her, she saw freedom slide away.

And then the unthinkable happened. The canoe reached the middle of the river, where the current was strongest. Though the sailor tried to keep heading for the far shore, the weight of all the passengers made the boat unstable. All those on shore watched in horror as the canoe tipped, spilling everyone into the angry river.

Catrine watched each one drown.

"I thought I was terrified at all that had happened already, but now I had little hope of living. Some of the remaining refugees chose to try the rope. Many lost their balance and were lost in the river. Others threw themselves into the water rather than being brutally killed by their enemies."

Several people pleaded with Catrine to cross on the rope, but what she saw scared her. And now the killers were in sight, also.

Suddenly another boat reached the shore. Trembling, Catrine stepped in. The journey across seemed to last forever, and when the current jostled the canoe, everyone screamed, sure that their fate would match the previous boat. But miraculously, they made it to the other side.

Burundi. A safe haven.

But the refugee camp held many of the same struggles of the journey. No food or water. Disease and death. No toilets. No shelter. Great numbers died each day—almost every single minute came the wails indicating another life was finished.

After several days of miserable survival, Catrine sat near the entrance of the camp, watching as more haunted and injured refugees stumbled in after crossing the Akagera River. Suddenly, she saw a familiar face.

"Mama!" she cried. Aunt Nzamugura fell at Catrine's feet, her face sagging with exhaustion.

"My dear Catrine," she cried. "I thought you were dead."

Aunt Nzamugura's two youngest sons were with her. Her two oldest boys had joined the RPF. Not because they wanted to fight, but they felt their best chance of survival meant aligning with the rebels and perhaps having a weapon with which to defend themselves. She had no idea if they or her other children were still alive.

Catrine wept to tell our aunt that her two daughters had been killed. They cried tears of joy and grief for being reunited, and missing their loved ones. Catrine was so relieved to have three family members with her again, and to have an adult to make decisions. But their situation was still desperate.

"With all the deaths, there was no burial place. Some people dug small holes or shallow pits to bury their relatives, but this was so painful to the family members—to see their loved ones buried in such disgrace. Not only that, but the bodies brought disease—cholera mainly. Others resorted to dumping their dead in the river, rather than bury them with dishonor."

Aunt Nzamugura had still been nursing her youngest daughter—one of those who were killed. She sat Catrine and her remaining two sons down. "There is no food. Each of you must drink from my breasts so that you have some nourishment."

The children took turns, from the youngest to the oldest.

One day, as they sat to nurse once again, Catrine had her turn. Immediately, she spit out a mouthful and wiped her lips with the back of her hand. She stared in horror at Aunt Nzamugura. Blood. All that was left in Aunt Nzamugura's breasts was blood.

"We can not do this any longer, Mama. It is not safe for you—or the rest of us."

Aunt Nzamugura's sunken eyes blinked slowly. "I will give what I have to see you all safe. Now drink. It is not much, it is not the best, but it is all I have to give." She became sick and grew weaker and weaker each day.

A few days later, when the sun began to rise, one of the boys shook Catrine awake. "Catrine. I cannot wake Mama."

Catrine moved to the still form of her aunt. Her chest lay unmoving. Aunt Nzamugura's face was relaxed, at peace. She had given her very life for her children.

"So among those who died," Catrine whispered, "was my darling aunt whom I loved with all my heart. I knew her as my mom. She loved me so dearly. Later on, my two little cousins died. This was the darkest moment of my life."

And so, the refugees who had survived machetes, clubs, knives, spears, sharp sticks, guns, and so many other tools of death, could not escape cholera and starvation.

Once the genocide finally ended, Catrine made her way back to her town, along with the scant people who had survived along with her. Even the journey home held dangers.

"Bloated bodies lay scattered everywhere. We had to jump over the dead and the body parts decomposing where they fell. If they could have been counted, the numbers would be unthinkable. Bodies rotted on the streets, in the bushes, in lakes and rivers, in houses, in toilet pits. But worst of all were the bodies in the churches."

Many people had fled to the Catholic or Anglican churches for refuge. But this decision proved fatal. Some priests and pastors willingly turned the desperate refugees packing their churches over to the killers. Some were slaughtered by machete or machine gun; other churches were set on fire to consume all those hiding within.

Exhausted from her tale, Catrine leaned back and closed her eyes.

I slid closer to Catrine, and laid my hand on hers—so, so lightly. My eyes closed, and the gathering tears slipped down my cheeks. A slight weight pressed into my shoulder, and I looked to see. Catrine was leaning her head on me.

With a deep breath, I praised God in my heart. And God kept his promise. He had told me his plan to bless those who hurt in ways far worse than I had experienced. Catrine's journey of healing had begun.

Secondary

IN EARLY 1998, after finishing primary school, I transferred to Luwero Secondary School, about fifty miles away from Uganda Gospel Rehabilitation Centre, and 150 miles from home. Saying goodbye to my dear friend Sebastian was not easy after all the time I had spent with him. Pastor David promised to stay in contact with me.

However, having reached the age of nineteen, I was more than ready to move out of primary school. Kindergarten and primary school combined normally take 10 years, but I had worked hard to complete everything in five years. Secondary would be another six years. Fortunately, Pastor David, and Lovie and Syvelle Phillips promised to visit me often.

In my new school, we were required to serve in some way. I was so eager to minister in that school. I worked on making friends and establishing relationships, and continued the youth ministry, conducting outreaches, conferences, and seminars. Sometimes ministry was challenging because I had to pray for someone to be willing to carry me on a bicycle to the farther locations. I started to visit four other schools every week in order to conduct Bible studies. The school also asked me to be Chapel Prefect of the secondary school, responsible for the spiritual life of the student body.

However, I confronted some issues after the move. My new black boots were two years old, and still invaluable to me. But living in the dorms here was much different from the way things were at the orphanage school.

Sharing bathrooms, toilets, sinks, and showers was a huge obstacle for someone unable to stand. Crawling on the floor in that situation was not an easy thing. Everything was made for those with two strong legs. Keeping clean was so important to me, yet it was not easy in those bathrooms used by so many students.

Finally, during that first year, I gathered my courage and spoke to the administration of the school.

"With my mobility issues and the format of the bathrooms, I am unable to maintain proper hygiene," I told them. "Could I have permission to rent a room in town to make this easier?"

Thankfully, the administration granted my request, and I found a room some distance away. This solved one problem, as I now had access to a bathroom on my own, but it caused another problem—transportation. Not only was the distance too far to crawl, but the school sat on a main road, full of speeding vehicles, making crawling dangerous. I hired a cyclist to ride me on a bicycle to school in the morning, and again every afternoon.

And the problem with the bathrooms continued during the school day. Most days I did not eat lunch, even though it was provided, as it just contributed to the need to use the bathroom. Likewise, I often left home in the morning without eating or drinking anything for the same reason. But I felt hungry. And crawling from class to class required energy. At last, I spoke to the administration again.

They were very gracious to let me use the staff restrooms, and it was much easier to manage. However, I felt somewhat embarrassed to go in there, as I respected my teachers greatly and they were so much older than me. I was just a student, and my instructors seemed so far above me, that it just did not seem right to go in there. So I still tried to go without lunch.

I threw myself into my studies and ministry, and God provided my strength.

Wheels

BUT THEN, NEAR the end of my first year in secondary school, when I was twenty years old, not one, not two, but three amazing things happened.

One day, during my time of prayer, God clearly spoke to my heart. *Canisius, you have asked for a wife. I will give you a wife.*

My heart swelled and felt like it could pop like a ripe melon. "Thank you, God!" I did not know how or when God would bring this to pass, but I trusted him completely.

On my next visit home, Catrine had wonderful news for me.

"My dear brother," she said, "I call you my brother not only because we share a mother and a father, but we now share a heavenly father. I am a born-again Christian!"

Already on my knees, I praised my God for his hand on Catrine, and the healing he had accomplished. Her journey was not over, but I was so thankful that she allowed my Jesus to begin healing her heart.

The third amazing thing was another miracle. A miracle that changed my life.

I received a wonderful wheelchair.

Two years before, Mama Lovie and Papa Syvelle had taken my measurements. They said they were collecting money in order to purchase a wheelchair for me. When a year went by and nothing happened, I tried to chase the excitement from my mind.

But now, the leadership of Luwero Secondary School came with a message. "The wheelchair has arrived in Kampala. We would like you to come with us to get it."

I could hardly sit still on the journey. A wheelchair! It did not seem possible. What would it look like?

When the box was opened, I just knelt there, stunned at the sight. My eyes could hardly believe what I saw.

Not a local-made wheelchair. Not something that would break with only a little effort. Not a chair made for just anybody. It was a chair made just for me. The quality surpassed anything I had ever seen in Uganda. Everyone gathered around to see this amazing sight.

One of the administrators rested his hand on my shoulder. "Canisius, Lovie and Syvelle told us they have seen the call of God on your life. They believe a chair like this can help you in your ministry."

Someone else added, "This wheelchair was made in America. And it was crafted just for your size."

"And it is purple!" I shouted. I crawled closer to examine it. It was so beautiful. The metal was shiny and new. Rubber tires showed the kind of tread that could get me places quickly.

"Lovie hopes you like the color," one man said. "They asked the factory to make it that way—a royal color—because they want you to always remember: you are a son of the King of Kings."

Someone on the edge of the crowd said, "This boy must come from a wealthy family. I have never seen such a wheelchair in my life. Look at him—the son of a rich man."

I smiled, thinking, "Yes, my heavenly Father is so rich, that he has given me spiritual parents who care about me."

Next, I found something on the back of the chair. "Look at this!"

"That's a bag to hold all your books as you travel."

The Phillips' generosity astounded me. They had raised the funds to purchase the off-road wheelchair for me. I couldn't wait to write them a long letter of gratitude.

That wheelchair helped me so much. It opened great opportunities at school. I no longer needed someone to ride me to school on the bicycle. Ministry opportunities at other schools, churches, and villages were more within reach. I had been crawling for twelve years. I thought, "I will never crawl again."

A new world opened up for me. The wheelchair unlocked my life.

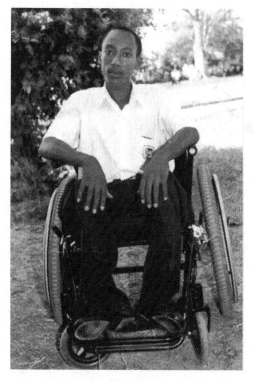

▲▼▲

Lovie and Syvelle visited whenever they could. I shared with them about my call to ministry and began to discuss the possibility of Bible college. Even considering the idea astounded me. For a boy who had waited so long for school, college seemed like a far-off dream.

"Could this really happen?" I asked. "Now that I have a wheelchair, this could be a wonderful thing."

Lovie's eyes twinkled. "Let us see what God can do. He placed this call on your heart, and he will make a way."

Lovie did not tell me that she took this project on as her personal mission. She began writing letters to several Bible colleges.

Meanwhile, I studied harder than ever and continued to devote myself to ministry in the school and in the community. And before long, I found a second opportunity that filled a deep longing in my heart.

Ministry to people with disabilities.

I was introduced to a man named Brother Jackson, a man who had a heart to minister to disabled people in Uganda like I did. He was part of a new organization called Great Hope for Disability Ministries. He had heard my testimony from people who knew me well. He watched as I conducted crusades and conferences.

"I feel you should be the chaplain of our ministry," he said.

There was nothing more I wanted to do than to minister to people suffering hardship as I had. This was the beat of my heart! So many disabled people were prisoners in their homes, kept hidden by their families. They felt rejected, not valued—like a nobody. I saw disabled people living in the streets, begging, smoking, doing drugs.

After praying about the decision for some time, I said yes to Jackson. I eagerly joined in with all my effort and became a member of the board of directors. The ministry kept me busy with counseling, conducting workshops, preaching, praying, and wheelchair distribution. Journalists came to write about what we were doing.

Back in the US, Lovie received some answers to her queries. The director of the first college said, "Because of his disability, the area where the Bible College is located is not in his favor. We cannot take him in."

Letters began to arrive from the two other colleges, one of them in Kenya. They began the same, "We regret to inform you . . ."

Lovie felt so disappointed.

During this time, I received an extra gift. Mama came to see me after we had been apart for ten years. And while we were together, I had the great privilege to pray with her to receive Christ.

Afterward, she gave me a big hug and looked into my eyes. "My son," she said, "I am your biological mother, but now I can say that you are my spiritual father. Your life speaks."

God gave me the privilege of leading many of my family to Christ.

▲▼▲

One month, Syvelle was invited to speak at a conference in Seguku, Uganda. He had spoken there before, and Lovie spent the time visiting schools and children's homes to speak to the kids.

While there, some close friends of theirs, Ron and Shirley DeVore, told them that they were planning to open a new Bible college right in that location.

"Wow," Syvelle said. "This might be a great opportunity for Canisius, and it's not so far away." The school was just a short drive south of Kampala, the capital of Uganda.

"Praise God!" Lovie smiled. "I know they'll take him. Ron and Shirley have heard us talk about him."

Lovie and Syvelle traveled to the school and spoke with the director.

He gave them an emphatic 'no'. "We can never handle him," he said. "You know what the terrain is like. The road going up to the classrooms is almost unmanageable even for a car when it rains. It's impossible."

"But you will love him!" Lovie argued.

The answer was still no.

The Phillips felt disappointed and wondered how God would provide for my schooling. But Lovie and Syvelle did not give up. They believed God would use me, and they prayed for God to make a way.

Not long after this, they heard that the director of that school had to return to the US after his wife became ill. The new director was a close friend of Lovie and Syvelle, Ed Pohlreich, who had met me on several occasions. They made another hopeful trip to the college.

"Absolutely," Ed said. "Canisius can come to our school. Even if it means to carry him on my back, I'm willing to do so."

Finally, there was a yes! When Lovie and Syvelle surprised me with the news, I could hardly believe it. What a time of rejoicing we had as we praised God for making a way, along with my graduation from secondary school at the age of twenty-three.

I liked the name of the college. Yesu Akwagala meant 'Jesus Loves You Bible College'.

But God began to teach me a lesson. Great opportunity does not ensure God's destiny. And on the other side of the coin, neither do closed doors determine God's will.

I have passed through closed doors. Sometimes, humanly, we ask questions. But the truth is, God has always got the best way. We don't know how things will turn out, but God's plans never fail.

However, my excitement about Bible college was short-lived. Once the rest of the administration learned that I used a wheelchair, they informed me that attending would not be easy.

"Our school is built on a mountain, and the dormitories are at the bottom. The path to the classrooms is very steep and will not accommodate a wheelchair. We are so sorry to tell you this."

I bowed my head at this discouraging news. Was God saying that he did not want me to study to become a pastor?

Challenges had been part of my life for so many years, and God saw me through each one of them. The suffering I experienced. The many years of crawling—of limitations.

I lifted my head and straightened my shoulders. Challenges would always come. If God had seen me through in the past, he would see me through again. I knew God would make a way.

College

ON THE FIRST day of class, I dressed carefully in pressed trousers and a smart white dress shirt. After gathering my books and notebooks, I wheeled outside to the road that led up the steep hill.

One of my instructors, Pastor Scott Volz, pulled up in his car. "Would you like a ride, Canisius?"

"Thank you, Pastor Scott," I said. I opened the door and slid from my chair into the front seat while he folded my wheelchair and stored it in the trunk.

My grin that day was probably bigger than anyone's. I leaned my head against the seat as Pastor Scott navigated the switchbacks up the mountain. A light breeze made the great banana leaves sway to the music in my heart.

At the top of the hill, he set my wheelchair on the porch of the chapel. Hmm. I stared at the set of stairs leading to the porch and sighed. I suppose I will have to do a little bit of crawling, I thought. I made a mental note to bring my boots with me the next day. Once in my wheelchair, I entered the chapel with joy. Later, I found I had to do some crawling to get into certain classroom buildings, but I focused on listening to my professors. Each morning that week, the same thing happened. Pastor Scott and his wife were so gracious to me and loved me dearly.

God had brought me so far from when I had been a poor boy crawling in the bush. Things were really turning around. The 'honeymoon' I experienced lasted one week.

▲▼▲

The mountain beckoned. The morning sun cast a golden, friendly light, highlighting the classroom buildings perched near the summit. Morning heat began to shimmer the view, but it looked beautiful to me. The ruts of the road winked back at the sun. A deep inhale pulled the fresh air into my lungs, scented with flowers and ripening bananas. My joy and excitement could not be contained.

"Thank you, Jesus. I praise you for bringing me here. What a wonderful day to be alive."

It was Monday, the second week of college. I had risen before dawn to have extra time to pray, then press every wrinkle from my white shirt, and polish my shoes back to a shine again. I rolled my wheelchair to the edge of the road, books, paper, and pencils tucked neatly in the pack on my lap. I scanned the building behind which Pastor Scott would come, hoping he might leave a few minutes early today.

Gratefulness for God's provision filled me as I waited. Finally, I could continue fulfilling more of God's plan for me. He had provided so much. My heart leaped as I glimpsed the car's hood nose around the corner. As he rolled closer, I lifted my hand, grinning. Pastor Scott waved, his smile matching mine—as he whirled past me.

My jaw dropped open as I watched the car wind up the twisting incline. Why did he not stop? Had I not been clear?

I lifted my eyes to the mountain again. The summit no longer beckoned, but loomed over me.

Where was God's provision now?

I sat there, waiting, hoping that another car would stop to carry me up the mountain. But his was the only one.

The time for chapel came and went. Surely someone would remember me after chapel, and come to retrieve me. But no one came. The cars had such a difficult time with the steep road, I knew better than to attempt the task in my chair. Finally, I turned back and rolled dejectedly into my room.

Tuesday dawned dark and cloudy, with heavy rain. Though I prepared myself and waited at the door, no one looked my way or caught my eye. Perhaps for my instructor, the idea of lifting my wheelchair into the car seemed too hard.

Well, I had been crawling for years and years. *That* was hard! Now that I finally had a great wheelchair, my crawling days were over. I had put in my time. God saw my dedication. Didn't he?

I pushed myself back to my room and lifted my body to the bed. Complaints about the administration and my situation filled my mind.

After a moment, a quiet voice spoke in my bitter heart.

My son, did you come here to be driven—or so I can train you?

"But how can I be trained, if I cannot even get to class?"

I brought you here that you can be trained to go and do my work. I have a plan in all this.

Conviction pushed the complaints from my heart. How had I forgotten my gratitude to Jesus for healing my heart and giving me purpose? I determined to crawl up the mountain the next day. And I did.

But sliding those boots over my knees felt like traveling backward. The journey up that trail was so hard, so steep, so long. Mud and roots clogged the path, and several times I slipped and fell, smearing my white school shirt.

Student after student passed me easily on the trail. "God bless you!" they called cheerfully.

The thought that kept me going was that someone would probably give me a ride back down. That might make up for having to crawl from class to class in my boots.

After one class, I saw Pastor Ed Pohlreich, the director. He was surprised I did not have my wheelchair. "I will get someone to carry you down," he told me.

My face heated. "No, Pastor Pohlreich. I will be fine."

But Pastor Ed brought a student from a classroom. "Roger will carry you down the mountain."

"No, really," I protested. "I don't need that."

But Pastor Ed lifted me off the ground and placed me on Roger's back. "Today I am breaking your pride. You must be carried."

Tears sprang to my eyes, and I felt so embarrassed. To be twenty-three years old and carried like a baby—it was too much.

When I reached my dorm, I made a decision. "God," I said, "even if it rains, even if the sun is hot, no matter what, I am going to school."

But the decision was hard. So hard. When I began, my journey was filled with complaints. "Why am I suffering? Have I not suffered enough without a wheelchair? And now I have one and I still have to crawl. Why should this happen to me?"

Why not you? The still, small voice replied. *Do you think you will be blessed when complaining? I have plans for your life. This time has a purpose. Did you come here to be driven, or to let me work in your life?*

I had gone through so much in my life. Pain, discrimination, depression, hopelessness—for years. This mountain felt like too much added to all those things. I struggled for the next three days.

"God," I finally prayed. "I surrender. Give me the grace to climb this mountain. If you want me to train at this school, give me grace not only to climb the hill, but to climb the hill with joy, not resentment. To serve you with joy. If I see someone walking on two strong legs, I will pray for him, and encourage him. If I watch someone drive by in their nice car, I will lift them up. I will never give myself an excuse to miss my classes again."

God was so faithful to answer my prayers. No longer did I feel jealous or resentful of the other students. The half-hour climb gave me plenty of time to pray about my life, my future, my fellow classmates and professors. Because of all I had been through, I was drawn to those who were in pain, or hurting, or disappointed, and prayed for many. All that time up and down the mountain for four years added up to a lot of prayer time!

I learned to plan ahead. I wore a jacket, even in the intense heat, to protect my white shirt. My boots protected my trousers. Generous students carried my books and my wheelchair. I left early enough to have time to wash myself and my boots when I reached the top.

Crawling to Bible college. This photo was taken years later, after steps had been built on some of the paths.

God was so generous and gave me grace in abundance. From that day on, I never missed class. Even when other students stayed in the dormitory due to intense rain, I set out crawling anyway. God's grace was sufficient for me in those four years. Some students told me I encouraged them when they saw me. They said, "If you can drag yourself, how can I miss class?" I worked very hard in my classes and thanked God for giving me a new perspective. A perspective where I took my eyes off my disability.

My college years began to fly by. I met so many wonderful people. I got to know the founders of Yesu Akwagala Bible College, Pastor Ron and Shirley DeVore. Like Lovie and Pastor Syvelle, they were so dedicated to ministry and loved me unconditionally, becoming like another set of parents. Papa Ron had owned a company back in the United States, but he and Mama Shirley gave up everything to move to Africa and live in a tiny container house. Ron's boldness impressed me. He didn't mind taking trips into the bush, and even sleeping outside. He was willing to go into places that even Africans were afraid to go. Ron and Shirley began an organization called World Outreach Ministries Foundation, or WOMF, ministering with churches, orphanages, schools, crusades, medical outreach, and prison ministry, besides the Bible college. They looked to expand the ministry into many African countries.

Pastor Steven Mayanja served as chairman of the board of directors of Uganda Christian Outreach Ministries, a division of WOMF. Sometimes he spoke to the student body. Pastor Mayanja's messages challenged me, and over time, we became friends. He was a great example to me, and I looked up to him and appreciated his vision for God's work. His prayer life was the greatest example. Pastor Steve left his nice house every day at three or four in the morning to pray. I sometimes found him praying and speaking in tongues in the church when I came to pray myself. His example prompted me to seek God more than ever.

After my first year, the previous director returned to the college. Carl Martin was the director who initially said no to my coming to Ycsu Akwagala. But despite that, we became very close during my time there. He loved me so intensely and called me his 'hero'.

Pastor David came to visit me on several occasions. He had followed up with me at my secondary school and now came to encourage me in my studies at Bible college. Though we were not related by blood, we had such a connection of the heart, and he taught me so much about godly leadership.

Of course, Mama Lovie and Papa Syvelle came when they could. They always stayed in the guesthouse, which sat on the mountain even higher than the chapel and classrooms.

By this time, my ability to climb had been honed, and I enjoyed racing them to the top.

▲▼▲

Ministry continued while I was at Yesu Akwagala. I was reluctant to step out of the youth ministry that I began back in primary school, and did not want it to stop. So I continued leading there. And I remained chaplain of Great Hope for Disability Ministries. I served in the church, sang in the choir, led the youth, and helped in the evangelism and conference departments.

Sometimes I received speaking invitations, and other times I visited villages to hold crusades. Though I could not use my wheelchair during the week on the mountain, it was so helpful for traveling to some of the ministry locations.

All these activities kept me busy every moment. My classes both thrilled and provoked my thinking, and I continued my study habits from primary and secondary school, working very hard to maintain my grades.

To have balance, I put God first. Then my priority was my education. Nights found me in extensive study. At times I went to bed at 2:00 am, and woke at 3:00 am to start again. I tried to be an example of a good student.

As time passed, my heart felt full to overflowing.

There was little chance for rest, but I kept up my habit of daily prayer also. One of those prayers concerned my wife.

I still believed what God had told me years before—that he would give me a wife.

Many beautiful and intelligent women attended both college and church, but I focused my mind away from those thoughts. God had brought me here for training, and I did not want to distract myself from that purpose.

When I saw someone who was let down or hurting, my burden to speak with them and comfort them rose from memories of how I felt before I found a relationship with God. The peace and love he gave to me through faith in him moved me to share that with others. I spoke with those in pain or disappointment, or even those who felt suicidal. To sit with them and listen and offer comfort gave me so much joy. But I did have to be clear when I listened to a hurting woman. I did not want to give her, or anyone else, the wrong idea. I let them know that I saw them as a sister. My own sisters were near their age, and I would not want a man to treat them casually, or plant a seed in their mind that would not be right. I focused on treating women with respect, and encouraging everyone I came across.

One day, I prayed, "God, you know I have been praying for my wife, my kids, my family since 1994. I am asking you that you would give me grace that I will marry by October of 2006." College would end in October 2005. Once

I was established in ministry of some kind, my thoughts could turn toward marriage. I presented this request to God and rested, knowing that he knew what was best for me. He made a way for me to be here at Bible college, and he would make a way even in this.

Decision

MANY TIMES, WE spend much time thinking that we are the only person who is facing a challenge. I know that at times I had this mindset, like when I struggled with not finding a ride up the mountain to class.

One day, I was invited to preach at a church. Many churches invited the Bible college students to speak, and on this occasion, I rode behind a friend on a motorcycle. On the way there I saw a disabled man, sitting in the middle of the road, begging. I had never seen anyone with a deformity like this man. He was so bent that you could hardly see his arms and legs. As we rode past, I turned my head to keep the man in sight as long as possible.

In my heart, I asked some hard questions. "Can I have the excuse of not serving God when I see someone in such a position? I could easily be like him, on the street begging. Don't I need to use what I have to serve God?"

This experience made me think deeply. Being self-centered is so easy. We want to gather our experiences around us, never going beyond ourselves. But if we do go beyond ourselves, we discover so many people who are in even more pain. God wanted to use me. If I could stop thinking about myself, he could use even my past painful experiences to help others. To bring to them the hope of healing that God had brought into my life. The choice of who to think about was up to me.

▲▼▲

In 2003, my second year of Bible college, the foreign missions director in charge of Great Hope for Disability Ministries and his wife approached me. "Canisius, we have seen your heart for the disabled. We have never seen passion like yours, and we have a proposal for you. We would like for you to start a new church—one with a great ministry for those with disabilities. We have put everything in place for you. You can start immediately."

They laid out the details, and my mouth hung open in amazement. They offered me a beautiful house, a big compound, and a fancy office. No one in my family had stayed in a house such as this one. As soon as the church grew, they would purchase a tent for us to meet in. They promised a car to deliver me to speaking engagements, and even a credit card with extra money on top of a salary.

I had such a heart for this ministry, and though I was serving as the chaplain, I was not sure that this particular church plant was God's timing or location. That was something to pray about.

Since I was able to move into the house they provided, I asked my dad if Catrine could come to live with me there. I missed her greatly, and I wanted so much to spend more time with her and help her grow as a born-again Christian. He said yes, and what a reunion we had! Catrine helped me with the meals, and I spent time discipling her.

The director had told me they planned to purchase land and begin the church in Kampala. The church would be for all people, but would welcome the disabled. On top of all that, the ministry had planned a trip for me to go to the United States. They made arrangements with thirty churches who were willing for me to come and speak.

The director said, "God is telling us that we need to begin this now, and you are the right person to lead this church."

My first thought was, "Say yes!" The decision would be so easy. It was such a great idea. God had been faithful, allowing me to be useful, allowing me to be someone. And allowing me to minister to people I understood.

But right behind those thoughts, came another one. "I need to know the heart of God."

And so I asked for some time to pray about the decision.

▲▼▲

The beautiful red flowers along the path up the mountain opened their petals to the sun as I crawled toward my classes. I felt as if my life was much the same—opening to the amazing opportunities God had in store for me.

I explained the situation to Catrine. "I know that God had given me a pastoral calling. But so far, I lack two things. The timing and the destination. I want to be sure of the place where God calls me to serve. Does he want me to plant this church? Every door is open in that direction. This is a great ministry. Exactly what I have been longing for!"

She smiled at me. "Why don't we pray about it again?"

What an encouragement my sister was to me.

And then I got down to prayer. "God, they have given me this opportunity. This is your way. I believe that."

I waited for God to speak, confident in his agreement with this plan.

My son, I never called you for that. If you plant this church here, you will leave people spiritual orphans.

My eyes blinked in surprise. "God, I thought this was you."

No. Just because you have an offer, does not mean that ministry belongs to you.

And so, I went to the foreign missions director and explained what God told me. It was hard to go back to the couple and tell them. "Thank you for your trust," I said. "I feel I do not have the go ahead."

They didn't believe me, despite my assertive tone. "Pray about it again please," they told me. "Take some time. If you don't accept, we don't have a plan B. We will scrap all of these opportunities."

A lump filled my throat, but I said, "I have walked with God for some time. And he is telling me he did not call me for this."

They kept calling, and we spoke for hours. Finally, I confirmed that I would not accept the pastoral position of this new church. "You are free to scrap anything if you feel convicted, because I did not ask for all these things," I said. "The vision God has given me is more valuable than all these wonderful opportunities you presented to me. My calling is different, even though this ministry seems perfect for me. I treasure what God is speaking to me. I will wait for God's leading. I know he will make a way."

Once they realized my 'no' was firm, they pulled all the privileges, and I had to end my participation in that ministry. When I moved from the house back to the college, Catrine had to return home. Despite all these things that seemed like setbacks, I knew God did not speak with two different voices. Even though this plan seemed ideal for me, I believed God had something else in mind.

I learned this through the experience: People can cause you to lose your vision. If you don't know the heart of God for your life, you can be misled. Before you make major decisions in your life or in ministry, I ask you to take ample time in the presence of God and allow him to speak to you.

▲▼▲

In Papa Ron's office, I had shared the vision for the disability ministry. He was one hundred percent willing to stand with me and make sure everything went well, and I was so grateful for his support. But still, I wavered.

During the following days, God really spoke to me, and he was very clear. There was something else he *was* calling me to.

Pray for Rwanda.

God brought a burden for me to pray intensely for the nation of Rwanda. I obeyed that instruction and knew that it was from God. But as I prayed month after month, the voice told me, *I want you to go to Rwanda and plant churches there.*

At first, I believed this instruction did not come from God because I felt so confused. To have an opportunity like the one I had just rejected, and then a thought about a place I did not want to go made me feel unsure. Besides, I had already talked to Pastor Ron about the other ministry. Perhaps I would sound indecisive.

I had no mind at all of *going* to Rwanda. It was against my wishes. Rwanda was a place full of pain and tragedy. Many of my family had died there. I had seen other people go to Rwanda and return empty-handed. I knew a few people like Pastor Isaac and Pastor Godfrey who had moved there to begin churches. Life in that place was not anything like Uganda. Uganda was easy, and I felt content and comfortable where I was.

One day, as I prayed, I cried in my heart. "God, give me a burden to pray for Rwanda as never before." I did not want God to send me there. But prayer? That I could do.

From then on, I began to pray for Rwanda at every opportunity. And with those prayers came an increasing burden.

Go to Rwanda.

Go there? Impossible. With my fingers, I ticked off the reasons a ministry in Rwanda would not work for me. Rwanda was expensive, whereas living in Uganda was cheap, according to those I knew who had returned from there. Though I knew the language, my accent would not translate well in Rwanda. I had no such issues in Uganda. In Uganda, when a church began, they were allowed to meet in a living room or a temporary shelter. These things were illegal in Rwanda. A new church was required to rent, buy, or build a building.

Most of my family lived in Uganda, along with untold numbers of friends. So many people I could count on, who I could call when I was in need, people who believed in me and recognized my call. Other than Pastor Isaac and Godfrey, I had almost no one in Rwanda. To me, it seemed clear that going to Rwanda could not work on so many levels.

I spent the next year arguing with God about Rwanda. I tried to convince him with all my excuses, but God did not agree. This brought me great worries and many unanswered questions.

"God, this is too hard for me. Don't you see my disability? I cannot go there and begin a ministry. Too many things are against me."

When I looked at both situations, it seemed that the disability ministry in Uganda had showed every open door. All I had to do was walk through. On the other hand, the unknown ministry in Rwanda revealed only closed doors. I didn't have money, or contacts, or even a location.

One night, I had a dream. I saw myself going to Rwanda. People came and grabbed me from my bed, and threw me down. They pulled me from the house where I stayed, hitting me with clubs and machetes.

When I woke up, I cried, "God, where are you sending me? Do you want me to be killed?"

My son, he said. *The best place for you to be in is where there is my will.*

Those words struck me with an incredible force.

God's will. That was where I longed to be. Even if it might be inside a cave, that would be the best place on the planet. The place where he would do his work, in his way, and nothing—not finances, or language, or laws, or connections could block what he chose to do.

I closed my eyes and bowed my head in submission. "God, if it is like that, I'm saying yes. Despite the fact that I have no money. That language is a barrier. That I barely know anyone. Even if it is a dangerous place. But I still need more confirmation. At least give me one sign." So many signs seemed to point toward ministry in Uganda, but I had nothing but God's voice in my heart to make me sure of ministry in Rwanda.

He had spoken to me, and I was sure of it. His voice was very clear. But I wanted a real confirmation that I was not being driven by my emotions or my thinking. Whenever I spent time in prayer daily, I made this request for a sign.

And then I had another dream.

In this dream, I saw the president of Rwanda. Workers were renovating a house, and the president was inspecting the workers' progress. I was sitting on a chair in the corridor, and soon realized this house belonged to the president. Someone picked up my chair and said, "Please go inside."

"No," I replied.

The man sat on the chair facing me. I discovered this was the president himself.

"Mr. President," I said, "Thank you so much for what you have done for the nation." For Rwanda had changed in a great many ways already.

He smiled. "Thank you for your prayers. Without your prayers, we could not have achieved this. Keep praying for us. Because God has said that we still have more wars to fight."

I held his gaze. "Mr. President, be very careful when people tell you that God has spoken. You have to realize and to discern and know whether it really is God who is speaking."

Then I woke up. And I heard a voice—audible this time.

The guidance of the nation belongs to you.

It was very clear. From that moment on, I had no doubt about God's call to Rwanda. I had been struggling with this decision for more than a year.

"God," I said, "Whatever comes, I'm willing."

▲▼▲

In July 2004, one of the Bible college directors, David Easterly, gave a message about vision in one of my classes.

At that time, I was struggling with how to go to Ron DeVore and Pastor Steve to share my decision. When I speak a word to someone, I try to be loyal to my word. I felt that switching my thoughts from the disability ministry to Rwanda made me seem like I was becoming a double-minded person.

"God, can you help me?"

That day, when Pastor Easterly spoke, he said, "If God gives you a vision, remember that God's visions are progressive. When God gives you a vision, it keeps on growing."

His words reminded me that I had come to Bible college with a vision. A vision to preach, among many other things. And God had been growing that vision in the last year. I had lacked the timing and destination, but God had made the destination clear, even though I did not know the specific place.

Pastor Easterly spoke much about vision, and in my heart I felt God wanted to use him in my life. After the message, I rolled my wheelchair to the pastor's office.

"Pastor Dave, I don't know how you are going to take me, but I felt like sharing my heart with you." I rolled a little closer. "I have struggled with this for a year. Because of what has been happening, I feel I am willing to pay any price. Whatever it will cost me, I am willing to do so—even if I don't get anyone to believe in me." And I explained what God had been telling me.

Pastor Dave folded his hands and smiled. "Canisius. I have watched you. I've stayed around you. I've known your heart. I know that your decision is godly. I feel that is God speaking."

One of the classes Pastor Dave taught that I had not taken yet discussed awakening our call and the idea of generational transfer—how blessing can be transferred to another generation. What if blessing could be transferred to another generation in Rwanda, a nation torn apart by violence?

I told Pastor Dave, "I am determined to go to Rwanda to see what is happening, to mark the land and spiritually map the place. And I know—when you ask me how—I know God will make a way."

"I will pray for you," he said, "and if God enables me, I will also support you."

Not long after, I found out that Pastor Steven Kaweesa was planning to go on a mission trip to Rwanda in October of 2004. Several people had signed up to go with him, but there was a cost involved. I felt God wanted me to go and scope out the potential for ministry, but I did not have the money for the trip. I shared the dilemma with Pastor Dave.

"Get another student to go with you and help you. I'm going to pay for your trip. You go there."

Scope

ON THE WAY to Rwanda, in October 2004, I did not share my heart about God's vision with anyone else in the group—that I was marking my 'promised land'. I kept that between God, Pastor Dave, and myself. But every step of the way, God kept sealing the word for me: *Rwanda*. Everywhere I went, I felt so strongly that this was where I belonged.

Several times I preached there, and people came up to me to say, "God wants you here."

But I didn't say anything to anybody. I just kept everything in my heart.

When I returned from the trip, I felt even more determined. I went to Pastor Steve Mayanja's office and shared the vision with him.

"Pastor, I don't know how you are going to take me. I don't know how you might see me. I don't know the kind of image you will get. But this is what is on the ground. God has spoken to me for this long time about going to Rwanda."

I hesitated, unsure of his response, yet I felt this was the time to speak. "You have been a spiritual father to me all these years. You have stood with us as students. The only thing I might need from you—more than anything else—is a spiritual blessing. And if you do that, that will be enough." I felt that a spiritual blessing was more important and valuable than anything else.

My heart was full of gratitude to God that he had enabled me, and had used so many people in my life. From the tender age I came to Christ, then the time I came to the orphanage, secondary school, and Bible college—men and women of God were used to speak into my life. Many people spoke hope, spoke destiny. I have treasured their example and instruction.

Pastor Steve and I had always had great interaction, and I often shared my heart with him.

Pastor Steve listened carefully, and I knew he would give me his honest opinion. "Canisius, if he is God, he will do it."

Next, I went and shared with Papa Ron. Right away he asked, "Where are you going?"

"I am going to Rwanda."

"Then how did you change your mind?"

It took a while to explain all that had happened since we had last spoken about my future. He also said, "If it's what God wants, go. If God is in it, go."

The year before, in 2003, I had received my diploma in Theology—the halfway point to my four-year Bachelor of Theology degree. At that time, my friends and family held a party for me and gave me many gifts, including two cows. I was determined to make a second trip to Rwanda, and now I had the means. I sold one of the cows to finance a trip in April 2005.

Long ago, I believed that cattle-keeping would be my livelihood. Now, cattle were providing the means for ministry. I smiled at the thought.

While in Rwanda this time, Pastor Isaac, my pastor from the time I followed Christ, invited me to his church in Kigali, the capita city of 800,000 people and growing. I remember arriving at his church on the back of a motorcycle and sliding my rubber boots on before climbing the stairs to the church.

For I had discovered that ministry in Rwanda had one additional drawback. After not being able to use my wheelchair to reach the classrooms at the Bible college, I was looking forward to using my wheelchair full-time again. But the terrain of Rwanda, and especially the city of Kigali was mountainous, with steep, rutted roads that were mainly unpaved. I would have to sacrifice my mobility for ministry.

Pastor Isaac had moved from Uganda to Rwanda after the genocide to begin ministering to the many people hurting in the aftermath. When I visited him, I had not shared with anybody in Rwanda that I planned to move there. We sat and talked, and prayed together.

Suddenly, Pastor Isaac said, "I have seen God bringing you to Rwanda." God had given him a vision, even as we sat there talking. "I have seen you coming to Rwanda. I have seen people undermining you, looking down on you. But I have also seen God giving you a great ministry. I see you raising up. I see you on the radio stations. I see you on the national television. I see God doing incredible work."

I just sat there and stared at him, for I had not shared anything of my heart with him. So then I told him what had been happening and how I had a clear vision. Though I had not been doubting the call, from that point on I never questioned that God called me to Rwanda.

▲▼▲

On that same trip, God confirmed the exact location. I reached an area in Kigali which is called Nyamirambo, which means 'the place of dead bodies' or 'the place of carcasses'.

That neighborhood had been on my heart during my first trip, but I had not yet visited there.

The stories and poems say that in ancient days, a great battle ensued between Rwanda and another kingdom. When the enemy attacked, they defeated the Rwandan soldiers and made camp on this spot. Though the remaining Rwandan soldiers retreated, they planned to retaliate when the other army rested.

The Rwandan soldiers surrounded the camp with heaps of dry grass, leaving only one entrance. After they lit the grass on fire, the fleeing enemy were cut down as they fled the flames. All the bodies were gathered in one place, and the king of Rwanda offered sacrifices here. And so, the area was named 'the place of dead bodies'.

And that was not the end of death in this place—the history of death and slaughter continued. This was the first place used for burials. Also, before the genocide, thousands of innocent people who were suspected of being rebels were gathered in the stadium there, locked in, and left to starve for weeks. And then, Nyamirambo was one of the places where people were killed in a brutal way during the genocide.

I heard the Muslim call to prayer, reminding me that this was the most staunch Islamic area in the whole city. Churches did not prosper here, but mosques did just fine.

As I studied more about the area, I discovered that it had a very high rate of crime. Alcoholism, AIDS, theft, gambling, prostitution, drugs—all those things were found in abundance. I could not have chosen a place that was more difficult to make a difference.

Yet God spoke. *This is the place.*

Everything I saw made me think, "This is too hard." But I remembered the Israelites after they left Egypt. Joshua and Caleb were sent with ten other spies to scope out the land God promised would be theirs. They brought back fruit and honey and other evidence that the land was a wonderful place.

But then the other ten spies started yelling and crying, and they said, "The land is so good, but the people are giants! We are like grasshoppers before them."

And I liked what Joshua and Caleb replied, "If the Lord is pleased with us, he will lead us into that land, and will give it to us."

If the Lord is pleased with us—that was so important. Paul says, "If God is for us, who can be against us?" And Romans 8:32 says, "He who did not spare his own Son, but gave him up for us all—how will he not also, along with him, graciously give us all things?" In other words, we have God's best, precious promises. If we embrace them and position ourselves, great things can happen.

And I couldn't wait to start.

▲▼▲

When I returned from that second trip, I shared all that happened with Papa Ron. He told me, "Son, if God gives us grace to stand with you, we will do so."

Now, I became bold enough to start sharing with more people. I remember going to one of the leaders and sharing my heart.

He said, "Brother, God has called other people to that land. You should stay here. God has not called you there."

This man was and is a good friend. Probably, he looked at my situation, and couldn't imagine how God could make a way. His words discouraged me somewhat, since I respected this leader so much, and valued and trusted his opinions. His words did not bring doubt, but just disappointment that likely my disability caused him to ask me to reconsider.

Years later, this same man came to visit me in Rwanda and spoke to the new church. "I'm so sorry," he said. "When Pastor Gacura came and said, 'I'm going to begin the church,' I doubted him. And I'm saying sorry, and please forgive me."

This man was such a blessing in my life. I learned that true success does not depend on what people say about you, but depends on how we hear and obey God's voice. God judges how we respond to his voice.

I planned one more trip in July to finalize things in Rwanda. I felt determined and full of purpose. Whether I found someone to support me or not, I was willing to go. Papa Ron stood with me and supported me. And so I went.

On this trip, I encountered some more issues. The words spoken by Pastor Isaac continued to be true. Some people tried to undermine me.

One pastor who I thought would help me, took me aside. "This is such a hard place," he said. "Why don't you think about coming and being an associate pastor here at our church? Nyamirambo is a too unfavorable. Don't go there."

Other people also counseled me against going to that part of the city. God had given me a mission, yet others who I expected to encourage me came repeatedly to tell me 'no'. These words left me feeling discouraged.

But I told them, "Please. God has spoken to me to come and begin this ministry."

After this trip, I visited my family. I shared with my dad what I was going to do, and asked him to allow Catrine to come with me and help me. He agreed.

Then it was time to talk to Catrine. "God is sending me to Rwanda. I would love for you to come with me, but I will understand if it is too painful to return to a place that caused you such pain."

"I am going," she said. "I am going with you. You are not only my brother, but you are like a father, a mother, my best friend, and my pastor at the same time. There is nowhere else I would rather be."

One day, I said to her, "Catrine, you have told me about the worst day of your life, during the genocide. Now I want to know what was the best day of your life."

Catrine squeezed my hand. "The day you came into my life. You showed me love and tenderness when I was so hurt and confused. You listened to me. You told me about God's love for me. You changed my life, my perspective, my destiny."

My dear sister, Catrine.

I also visited Pastor David and told him, "I need your blessing." I went to my secondary school pastor, Fred Kiwanuka, and he prayed a blessing. I visited Pastor Steve Mayanja, and he did the same. I spoke with Papa Ron DeVore, and he also blessed me.

And then I went to one of my heroes—Papa Syvelle Phillips. When he and Mama Lovie came to visit, I told him, "I need a fatherly blessing from you." Papa did so. It is hard to explain how much that meant to me—to get a blessing from my spiritual parents. They believed in me when no one else did, when others saw me as useless. From this time, I was very sure I was on the right track. I knew God was going to stand with me. I knew God was going to defend me. No matter what, I was willing to pay every price.

Lovie and Syvelle spoke to the DeVores about me. "Could you let Canisius be a part of World Outreach Ministry Foundation?"

The DeVores agreed. Pastor Ron said, "Both of us feel like his parents. But we are two sets of parents without competition."

When Pastor Ron had preached at our graduation that October—a great message—one of the things he mentioned was this. "If God is calling this guy, we are willing to send him and support him financially to go and to be a missionary in the nation of Rwanda." He challenged the audience. "You—what are you doing? Where is God sending you?"

During one of the church services at Seguku Worship Center, Pastor Steve Mayanja called me up and prayed a blessing over me. The entire church blessed me. It had been my heart's cry that if I was going to begin the ministry, I would get a blessing from my spiritual parents. And God heard my prayers, for all my spiritual parents blessed me

So Catrine and I loaded everything and moved. The new adventure had begun.

Daddy and Mama at my Bible college graduation.

House

AS I ALREADY understood, new adventures are not easy. My adventures of mobility, my time at primary and secondary school, my time in Bible college—all these brought both challenges and blessings.

Rwanda was no different.

People often assumed I was a beggar because I crawled. Sometimes I entered a store to buy something, and the owner would toss me a coin and ask me to leave. Buses were not accessible to me at all. When it was time to hail a taxi, the process could take hours, as the drivers imagined that I was just going to beg for a free ride. The few that were willing to stop asked me to pay a fare for my wheelchair, if I had it with me. I finally had to resort to hiring motorcycles to take me around, but this required leaving the wheelchair at home. These incidents reinforced how the disabled were treated in Rwanda.

Catrine and I spent three weeks in the home of Pastor Godfrey and his mother. This was a little like a homecoming, for Godfrey's mother was none other than my grandmother's sister, with whom I had lived for a time in primary school. We came to Rwanda in November of 2005 and immediately began searching for a place to live.

I had a little money, but not much. And during those three weeks, we had to keep putting gasoline in the car we borrowed to go and see the different options for housing in the Nyamirambo area. The terrain was too rough for me to manage in the wheelchair. Everything was so expensive, and I watched my funds dwindle. I had ordered a bed, as none of the houses had furnishings, so I knew I needed to save a certain amount to pay for it.

One day I counted what I had left. Only 15,000 Rwandan francs, the equivalent of twenty-one US dollars. I knew I needed to support my sister—she had not been in ministry like me. I didn't want to tell her that the money was almost gone, and yet I didn't want to impose on our hosts more than we already had. Besides, I was itching to get started with doing what God called me to do. And for that, we needed to be in the Nyamirambo neighborhood.

Finally, we found a house in the right area, the cheapest one we could find. It had a large living room with an adjacent dining room—perfect for a house church, as I did not have money to rent a hall. I spoke with the owner.

"Yes, the house is available. The rent for this house is 40,000 Rwandan francs, about $56 per month. I will need six months of the rent in advance."

My throat went dry. I had only a fraction of *one* month's rent, let alone six months. I said nothing to Catrine on the way back to Godfrey's house.

Once there, I sat down with them. "Thank you for hosting us and extending your hospitality, your love, and your care. But tomorrow we are moving to the new house. We are shifting from here and going there."

Pastor Godfrey's jaw dropped. "You have money?"

I didn't answer, but rolled to the guest room, dropped to my knees, and prayed. "God, you have spoken to me. I know you sent me here. I don't have enough money to do what you have called me to do. If you have sent me here, show me the sign that you are with me."

When I finished praying, I felt so much joy. I knew God was going to take care of it. I came out and told Catrine it was time to pack our things. I called the owner of the house.

"Tomorrow we would love to move in. We will give you the money when we enter."

Then I said, "God, now it's your turn."

Afterwards, I felt an urge in my heart to check my email. I asked Pastor Godfrey to drive me to the internet cafe. An email was waiting from Lovie and Syvelle. They had written a wonderful letter.

"Son, we feel the Lord has led you to begin the ministry. We feel the Lord has led us to bless you with this amount of money to help you with what you want to do for the kingdom."

They had sent $1800 US dollars! I could not believe that. I had to blink and asked Pastor Godfrey, "Would you read this and see what I am seeing?"

He read, "We have sent this money through Western Union. $1800 US dollars." His face lit up with excitement.

We withdrew the money right away, and I felt uneasy carrying such a fortune in my pocket. This amount converted into 800,000 Rwandan francs at that time, far more than we needed for the six months rent. God's answer was beyond my imagination.

That miracle was something which has encouraged my life. When I get to a place where things seem impossible, that miracle encourages me. I sometimes remind God, "You intervened on November 27th, 2005. I know you have plans, so if you intervened then, you can also intervene in this situation." God's provision was another confirmation that he was there for me.

God does not need our strength—he needs our obedience. Obedience is more than enough. What is foolish to the world means everything to God. Like in the Bible, David's obedience to his father telling him to check on his brothers led to David's victory over the giant. That one step took him to Goliath. David never went back to keeping sheep again.

Obedience makes things happen.

So Catrine and I moved into the house. It had nothing but our beds and the things we brought. I used some of the money from the Phillips to purchase some benches and chairs. I could have furnished the whole house in a nice way, but I wanted to be very careful with the money God provided.

On December 5th, we started going door to door, talking with the neighbors, and in the evening we did a crusade. Pastor Godfrey sent a group of his people to help us with the crusades. Some of the people must have thought it strange to see a pastor who crawls, but I knew they would see God's power if they were watching what we were doing.

Now the house I rented was far up a steep hill, like the Bible college. Due to erosion on the dirt roads, there were deep ruts, and the grade was so steep cars or motorcycles could not manage it. The incline was too much for my wheelchair. We had to leave the car we used at the bottom of the hill and leave the wheelchair in the house.

I resorted to the rubber boots again.

Catrine asked, "Are you discouraged about crawling again? You had to crawl for four years at the Bible college, and now you are crawling again at the age of twenty-seven."

"You know, Catrine," I said. "When I came here to Nyamirambo, I realized why God allowed me to climb that hill to the Bible college for four years. Why people did not give me a ride. God was preparing me for this place."

If I had not had that training, I could have complained or given up. But my God sees far beyond our imagination. He trained me so that I could go to Rwanda and crawl without complaining. God knows how to turn what we thought our worst days into our best days. I was happy to sacrifice my wheelchair for the sake of the gospel.

Our trials now can be God's training for the future.

▲▼▲

Coming to Rwanda, Catrine and I found many hurting people. Some had physical wounds from the genocide— scars, missing limbs, AIDS, and more. Others had emotional wounds—post-traumatic stress disorder and grief from losing so many family members. But still others experienced a different kind of wound—shame and guilt for having been convinced that their neighbors must be killed.

Some people in this Muslim area had family members who participated in the genocide against the Tutsi. So much hurt and pain existed in this place of death. Sometimes a father had killed his own children because their mother was from the other tribe.

We did not want to name our church Nyamirambo—the place of dead bodies. We named our church Nyabugingo Worship Center, which means 'life-giving worship center'. The place of death would be turned into the place of life—eternal life. Jesus said, "I came to give them life, and life in abundance."

I realized that when I longed to minister to the disabled, to give them hope and acceptance, I was thinking far too small. God knew that those affected by the genocide—from both sides—dealt with the same issues. God's vision was far bigger than mine. And so I determined to minister to both those affected by the genocide, and the disabled, using the compassion God had forged in me, and the gentle weapon of God's love.

Our little church in the living room was illegal, but God had provided this house for his work. "God," I said, "if it is your business, you will protect this church. If it is not your business, they will stop it. I am going to do my part, and you do your part. My part is to do what you told me to do. Your part is to protect us."

And so we went on. It was not easy. The police came several times. "You have to stop immediately. You are causing insecurity in the area."

"Look," I told them. "We are not going to stop. We are not causing insecurity, but security. Do you think I'm trying to milk money from these people? I was once walking, like you. But life changed. No treatment could make me walk again. But I am here to speak hope to these people. Give us that opportunity, allow us to work. If we fail to do that, then you will come and stop us. But we have a vision. God told me to come here. I'm doing something to help my people—speaking hope, speaking life, serving God. I want to share God's word, which brought healing for my pain. I want to share my heart."

The policemen listened, and I spoke what I felt in my heart. "But you, instead of helping me, supporting me, asking me how you can help—you have the guts to come and stop me. You may be able to do that, but you will never stop God. This is God's business."

They were not the only ones to oppose us. Three things were against us: that the church was in the living room—which was illegal, that the pastor was a disabled person, and that I was not yet fluent in the Kinyarwanda language.

In all these things I had to believe and trust God.

The third week of December was a memorable time for the small Nyabugingo Worship Center. Pastor Steve Mayanja arrived with a team from Uganda to open the church officially—even though it was in the living room, and would remain there for more than a year. Their presence and support were a huge encouragement. At that time I was doing almost everything myself, but still we persisted.

I had been praying for land for our church for some time. On December 29th, 2005 God spoke to my heart, *I have given you the land.*

This word was hard to believe because even having money to buy food was a hardship. But I made an announcement to the church. "Be happy everyone! God has given us land."

Now it was time to locate the land God had provided. Soon I found a vacant piece of land in the area. Though the steep hills to reach it would make things harder for me, I praised God.

At church, I shared what I found. "Come see our land!" I said.

We all went to the property and laid hands on it, praising God. Yet we didn't know if the owner was selling it, and had no money to make a purchase. We later learned the property would cost $20,000—a staggering sum. But we believed God.

I told the congregation, "If God spoke to us about this land, he will make a way. He has made a way in so many other areas. Our God can be trusted."

Allen

DURING ALL THIS, God was working on another level—one that I was not immediately aware of. God had a special surprise for me. During my second trip to Rwanda the year before, when I was invited to speak in Pastor Isaac's church, I did not know that my future wife, Allen, attended there. She was a greeter at the entrance, and was standing on the steps.

Someone had driven me to the church on a motorcycle. I climbed off the motorcycle onto the ground and slid on my rubber boots. Then I crawled up the steps into the church.

I had no idea that the moment I crawled off the motorcycle, Allen heard a voice in her heart telling her, *That is your husband.*

She immediately refuted the voice. "In Jesus name, he is not the one."

She had heard of me from Pastor Isaac, how I was serving God. She had been praying for the right person, but didn't expect the rubber boots, and had never seen anything like a crawling pastor before.

At times, God challenges our mindset. He says, "My ways are not your ways." We find ourselves in a conflict zone when we are trying to match our way with His ways, wanting everything to be in our favor. Yet God knows the best for us.

For me, I didn't think anything about Allen as I crawled past. I had come for a mission to preach and had no idea of her conflict with God and the battle going on in her heart. But soon that battle would become mine, also.

Pastor Isaac, his wife, and I continued our close relationship. By the time I began the church in the living room in December of 2005, they stood with me in everything. Now Allen was a worship leader in her church. Pastor Isaac offered to send two worship team members to help me every Sunday until I found what I needed among my own church members. Allen was always one of those two.

For two months, Allen did an incredible job leading praise and worship. We did not have instruments then, only our voices. Our church began on December 5th, and Allen continued to help through the end of January, when we found members who were able to help.

As 2006 started, I thought back to my time in Bible college, when I had asked God to allow me to be married by October 2006. As that time was less than 10 months away, and I was busy with so many struggles and financial issues, I wondered if marriage would have to wait.

Yet I kept praying for God to show me the right person. I didn't want to jump in ahead of God. I prayed more and more. One day, a voice inside me said, *Don't you think Allen is your wife?*

I said, "No!" and stopped praying immediately. I blamed the voice on my emotions and thoughts. This bothered me a great deal. However, whenever I prayed again about marriage, the voice always came back. Before long, I stopped praying about marriage altogether because this voice disturbed me so greatly. Finally, I had to make a decision. I asked God, "Is it you? Are you the one doing this?" Yet the voice continued prompting me.

At one point, I shared the situation with Catrine. She said, "For sure, I think Allen might be the right person."

Part of my struggle was due to my position. Pastor Isaac had been so faithful, sending her to lead worship—the best he had—and I worried that my interest might seem a betrayal of my dear friend and pastor. I did not want to be seen as unfaithful, or taking advantage of someone he had sent. I longed to be sure it was a godly idea. Allen had genuinely served us with all her heart, without any false motives. She was entrusted into my hands, so could I express an interest in marriage?

My thoughts went back and forth. I wanted to retain my integrity before her pastor—and before her, and I knew she did not know me well. So I kept fighting the idea. I thought it might have been my own plan, and not from God. I knew God would give me the freedom of choice, but I longed to be connected with him in this important decision.

To make matters worse, I was discovering some interest from other young ladies. Some approached me directly, while others conversed with me in such a way that I was aware of their interest. Sometimes friends and relatives introduced me to ladies they knew who were available, whispering, "Please talk to this one."

These ladies were beautiful and educated, and sometimes I gathered my strength to speak to them. But inside, the voice reminded me. *No. She is not the right one.*

God continued to deal with me on the issue, getting my attention. I resolved that I didn't want to lead myself. I wanted God to lead me. I had tried my way, but that was not his plan.

One day, in January 2006, I prayed and said to God, "I want you to lead me. If I speak to Allen's pastors and they say something about her without my bringing up her name, then I know you have a hand in this."

So I prayed, and I approached Pastor Isaac and his wife. I never mentioned Allen at all. I said to them, "You've been around for some time, not only in your church, but different places. I have prayed for my wife for over twelve years. I am raising up for a ministry, and I want to maintain my testimony of integrity. I need a godly woman who will enable me, and who will join hands together with me to do this precious work God has given us. If you know of some young ladies I should consider, please share their names."

They told me, "That is a hard thing. We have so many beautiful, educated young ladies in our church, and there are more in other places. But finding a godly woman is a different thing. We know many people, but we have only one person who we can recommend to a genuine servant of God, and who is so dear to us. We have watched this young lady. We do not say that she's a super-human, she is a human being as others are, but she has got a godly character."

My heart began pounding in my chest. Are they going to mention another person? And I thought, Let it not be Allen. It's funny how I can laugh about all this now.

Then Pastor Isaac said, "This person is not any other than Allen."

In my heart, I said, "God, Allen again?" To Pastor Isaac and his wife, I kept my face expressionless. "It's ok, I will pray about that." I never let them know I had been thinking about her, and never showed them what I had in my mind.

I returned home, yet the issue kept haunting me. It seemed strange that Pastor Isaac or his wife never followed up and asked me what happened when I prayed about Allen. But even though they didn't follow up, God followed up. The situation got to the point where I stopped praying about a wife, because whenever I went to pray, the same voice told me, *But the answer is there. Allen is yours.*

Repeatedly, I said, "No." And I moved on to pray for other things, so I could put my prayers for a wife to the side.

The end of February came, and I had not seen Allen for about a month, since we did not need her anymore on Sunday mornings. We were about to host a conference at our church, and who came to lead the worship for that event? Allen. She and I had never sat down to talk beyond a hello or goodbye. She was teaching me a new song for the conference. I felt that it was time to find out if she was really the one for me.

Covenant

I TOOK A deep breath and sat her down. "I would like to ask you a few questions," I said. I asked about her life, what she thought about marriage, and whether she had prayed about marriage. My goal was to discover if she might have someone she was promised to. If she was already in a relationship, I did not want to interfere or come against another person, so I had to know.

In my ministry so far, and even back into Bible college and high school, I had many times counseled young people who made promises to one other, and then changed their mind. I was very aware that Allen might be in a similar situation.

"Is there anyone to whom you have made a promise of marriage?" I asked. I held my breath for her answer.

She looked down in a shy way. "I don't have anyone. So many people have come, but I have not said yes to any of them."

So I finally knew that she was free of other obligations. What a relief!

For the next several days, I prayed and thought about Allen constantly. I said, "God, what can I do?" I felt so restless that finally I had to call her. We met together at the church for our second-ever conversation. She taught me a new worship song for the service that night, and after singing that song, I wrote down the words. Then I knew it was time to talk to her.

I felt like I had to pick up my guts as a man. I didn't know what she would think of me, and that made me nervous. I worried that because she trusted me as a pastor, my interest in her would seem out of place. She was only 23, and I was 27.

"Ok," I said, swallowing. "You know what? I have taken some time. I don't know what you will think of me, or how you will view me, but I have observed you. I've prayed a lot about this decision, and what I'm going to ask you." I straightened my shoulders. "I would love for you to become my future wife."

Her eyes opened very wide.

Was her reaction good or bad? I did not know, but I kept going. It was time for all these words to be spoken. "I'm not going to tell you that this is what God spoke to me. I'm not going to impose on you that you must say yes." Was I being too serious? I forced a smile. "I want you to take your time. I want you to think about it. I want you to pray about it, and make a decision. The only thing I want from you is a yes or a no. You might give me the answer today, or you might give me the answer another time. I made a decision that this year I am getting married. If it is not you, then God has someone else in mind." I hurried to finish. "I want you to feel the freedom to think about this. You don't know me well. I may look funny to you. Just take your time and give me the answer, yes or no."

Allen sat very still. Then she said, "Ok. I'm not ready to answer now. I will take some time. You took your time and prayed about it. I need to see what will happen."

We talked a little while longer, then I had to ask, "Do you still see me as a pastor? Do you still trust me as a servant of God?" I felt very small, as if I had betrayed her trust.

She looked at me very seriously. "Yes, I do."

Then we prayed together, and we parted.

And that day, she led the worship. In the evening, she had to go back home. It was distressing, not knowing when she would give me an answer.

But before she left, she came to me and said, "Within a month, I will give you my answer."

During that month, the waiting felt like years. Yet I believed God was in control. I determined that if she said no, I was not going to argue with her. She did not belong to me. But if she said yes, how wonderful that would be!

At the end of the month's time, I arranged to meet her at a nice restaurant. I slept well the night before, firmly convinced that God was trustworthy, no matter the outcome. He had been faithful to me all these years already. Why should I doubt him now? He had given me the longing of my heart to read the Bible. He had provided entrance into Bible college. He had faithfully directed me into ministry in Rwanda. Why would he fail to guide me in the choice of a wife?

Allen looked so beautiful in a nice-looking skirt and blouse, with her hair fixed in a lovely way. The sight of her filled me with quiet joy, and I tapped my foot, trying to be patient for her answer. We ate a good meal of beef, chips, and salad, and talked about this and that. I learned that her father had been killed after he joined the RPF to help end the genocide.

Finally, we came to the main issue--the reason both of us were there.

"Last time," I began, shoulders tense, "I presented my idea to you, and now we are meeting again. I am eagerly awaiting your answer."

In my most assertive tone, I continued, "Please, for me, if you tell me yes, I will go with your yes. If you tell me no, I won't argue. You are free to choose. You are a beautiful young lady, and you have ideas of your own. Perhaps you have a list of what you are looking for in a husband, some qualifications, or preferences in appearance. So please, give me your yes or no, but not something in between."

Finally, forcing my shoulders to relax, I sat back in my chair.

Then she took a breath. A big breath. In her lovely voice, she said, "I have taken my time. I have prayed. I have tried to follow up on this idea. But now, I am saying yes."

Relief and joy poured through me, and a big grin stretched my face. I wanted to jump up and shout. But I forced myself to think twice. She might have made her decision for the wrong reasons, and I needed to be certain. So I reined in my emotions, and said to her, "Thank you, Allen, for that step. But I want to ask you some questions, which are very sensitive. This decision to marry will affect both our lives for the rest of our years together. We are sitting here in this restaurant, but we are doing something of great importance. We are making a covenant between us before anyone else is aware. So, I want to be sure—did you mean your yes?"

Allen blinked, seeming surprised. I hurried to explain.

"Allen, God is a witness before us, between you and me. I want to know why you said yes. Because even if you meant your yes, you are free to change your yes to make it no."

Her brows came together in thought--or confusion.

"You see, Allen, you do not know so much about me, the guy you are agreeing to marry. I want you to be sure. This is a guy who crawls everywhere in rubber boots. He doesn't walk like everyone else. This is a guy who conducts a church in the living room. This is a guy who has nothing, apart from what you see in front of you. I have no guarantee of success, of money, of position. The way you see me now, this is how I am. You do not know my family, but that is ok. The person you see is the one."

She opened her mouth to speak, but I lifted a hand. "Please, I have a few more things to say, and then I will listen in return. Just as I have no guarantee of success, I do not know when God might provide a place for our church that is not in the living room. Even if he doesn't do that, are you still willing to marry me?

"And even more important. I know you believe in miracles the way I do. You might think, 'Probably on our wedding day, Canisius will rise up and walk.' I believe God can perform that miracle even as we sit here. But if he doesn't do that on our wedding day, or if he never does, will it affect you? If I never walk again, are you still willing to marry me?" I thought that if Allen came into our marriage with expectations of success, status, or healing, she might become frustrated.

She took another very big breath with eyes wide, thinking through all these things.

My hope was not to discourage her, so I told her, "I want to be realistic, to be true to ourselves. I never want you to think that I deceived you, or led you to believe things will happen for certain, when they might not."

Finally, I held my hand out, indicating I was finished speaking. I felt deflated of energy, as I had spilled out all these things that might cause this lovely woman to change her decision. Still, my spirit was at peace.

Allen gave me a small smile. "Thank you for those questions. They are not what I expected, for sure. But I will tell you this. I am saying yes to you, not because of any other thing. I am accepting you the way you are. You did not come to me walking. I accept you the way you came." She shifted in her seat and met my eyes directly. "Why did I accept you? For my whole life, I prayed, 'God, bring me someone who is special. A special person.' He did that for me. And no wonder! The way you move is special. Your everything is special." Her smile widened so that her teeth glowed in the dim light of the restaurant. "I believe you are the right person. I asked God to give me a handsome man, and so you are. I asked God to give me an educated man, and so you are."

My hands trembled at the joy her words brought, and I clasped them together. "One last question, Allen. Is there anybody pushing you to say yes to me? Did you get the idea to say yes in a dream?"

With a raised chin, Allen answered confidently. "I never dreamt about this. I feel this decision confirmed in my heart." She didn't look away. "And because I love you."

My energy came flooding back, and I felt like I could circle Kigali City in my rubber boots. "Ok," I said. "That's all I wanted."

Then from that day, I told her, "I am ready for you. I'm ready to go along with you. We are going to become like Jonathan and David, or Ruth and Naomi, who said, 'your people will be my people' and 'wherever you go, I will go'. This is God's will for us, more than one hundred percent sure."

So even at that restaurant, we began to arrange all the details of our wedding. I had already planned the date, September 16th, 2006. We set a time to go and meet the parents, a time to meet the pastors, and a date for the introduction, which is similar to an engagement party. We planned everything in advance.

▲▼▲

But though we made our plans with much joy that March day, we both dealt with hardships in the month ahead. Though Allen was filled with joy at God's provision, not everyone shared in that joy.

Some people in her family and in her church were disappointed in her decision. These people had watched her grow up and become a woman of God, and they naturally wanted the best for her. To some, a poor, crippled pastor with a fledgling church in the living room didn't look like God's best. Allen faced a lot of questions. And those questions brought back feelings that reminded me of the days when I was recovering from polio, listening to people talk about me who didn't believe in me.

Why should a beautiful young lady go for such a person, they wondered. Perhaps she is miserable. Can she get no one else? Maybe no one ever proposed to her, and she felt desperate to say yes to the first person who approached her.

The elders of her church even sat her down and asked many questions. "If you marry this man," they said, "within one month, you will pack your bags and come back." They thought that perhaps Pastor Isaac had pushed her to say yes. Allen and I met with the pastors and shared how we had taken time and prayed before making the decision.

One man related to her said, "You do not even understand the decision you are making. That man is like a graveyard. How can you make such a foolish decision? After a few days, you will feel shame and regret."

With all these questions going on, I wondered what Allen's mother would think. She lived several hours away. Allen went to see her and brought some photos of me to show her. Allen's mother had beautiful words waiting for her.

She said, "My daughter, I have watched you. You have walked with God, and you have been faithful. You have not made me ashamed. Your father was taken from you when you were still young—and I nurtured you as a widow. You and your sisters became good girls, and made me proud with your choices." She smiled at Allen. "You are getting this man, who is a man of God. I'm just blessing you to marry him."

Allen's mother spread out her arms. "Go. This man cannot walk. Go and become his legs. Reach for him, where he cannot reach. Do what he cannot do. And my blessings are with you."

When Allen had received the blessing from her mom and the blessing of her pastors, she said to me, "Whatever comes, I'm ready for it."

▲▼▲

During these weeks of planning, Allen and I did not share our news with everyone yet. We wanted to wait until our official 'introduction', similar to an engagement party. This is the time that the families get together, and a ring is given. With all the challenges Allen already had with people who opposed our marriage, we chose to wait to share the news until everything was settled.

In advance of the official introduction, our families met to discuss the terms of the marriage. I met Allen's mom, and members of my family in Rwanda spent some time together with Allen's family, so we could know each other and feel comfortable with one another. All the plans were discussed for the introduction, the dowry, and the wedding.

Yes, I paid a dowry for my wife. This is something that has been in our culture—not as a payment for a person—but an appreciation gift to the family. They raised her. They helped her to become the woman she is today. So we show respect and thanks to the family for all they have done.

These negotiations are very important, because each family does things differently, so we initiate conversation and talk about the wedding plans, the dowry amount, any debts that are owed. Fortunately, we owed no debt. Both families engage with one another and come to an agreement, so there will be no future conflict between the families.

Some might think traditions like this strange in these modern times. To make so much preparation and effort, when it could be easy to say, "Let us get married today. Forget all these other things." But in Rwanda, that kind of situation is rare. Not only that, but a hurried wedding is not appropriate. For a woman to be given to a man like that, without an official giving away by her family, there would be the worry that he might not value her. All these preparations reveal to the future husband how treasured a woman is to her family. They will not allow just anyone to come and grab her, without knowing that this is an upstanding man, who will cherish her.

Finally in April, the day of introduction arrived. Allen and another pastor came to our small church in the living room. In my church, no one apart from Catrine knew about the introduction. When the pastor announced our impending marriage, everyone was surprised. Among the ladies they expected me to marry, Allen was not on the list. People started shouting with joy.

After that, we went to Allen's church and her pastors conducted the introduction again. In this way, we avoided any rumors that might start, and shared the dates of all the events, so that no one could bring opposition.

Then we held a big celebration to rejoice that we were pledged to be married. Both our families came together for a great party. More than 400 people attended the event. Allen officially introduced me to her family on July 1st, 2006, and I presented her with a ring. This is the time that the dowry is actually paid, having been settled in the previous family meeting. Next, we had to go for a civil marriage, which is very important according to the national laws in Rwanda.

Then all we had to do was wait until the official church marriage, scheduled for September 16th, 2006.

People began hearing about the wedding of this young lady and the guy in the wheelchair. So many of them wanted to become part of the event. Some said, "Even if you never invited me, I'm going to come." It was wonderful that people wanted to share our joy.

Allen and I continued to be amazed at God's love and the plans he had for us. II realized that if I had not come to Rwanda, I would not have discovered my amazing wife.

Provision

PRIOR TO OUR wedding, Allen and I visited Uganda so that she could meet my family and we could be introduced at Pastor Steve Mayanja's church. During the visit, Pastor Steve called me into his office.

"I have news for you," he said, unable to stop grinning.

"What news do you have?

"Through World Outreach Ministries Foundation, someone has heard your story about crawling to Bible college. God gave this person a burden to buy the land for the church. They gave an anonymous gift of $20,000!"

What an amazing God we serve! He gave us the money for that wonderful land.

Not long after that miracle, another amazing thing happened. On one of his visits before our marriage, Papa Ron and Pastor Steve Mayanja came to visit at the house where Catrine and I lived.

"This house is too tiring for you to reach." Tears filled Papa Ron's eyes. "You are having to crawl like a dog. Find a better house, and I will help you with the rent."

Papa Ron's kindness filled me with such joy. "Thank you, Lord," I prayed. "For you have seen my faithfulness all this time and you are making a way for me." And just in time for my wedding.

So I prayed about the possibility of a different house, but God was very clear. *If you move from this house to another house, the church will not work in the new location.*

I had a choice: listen to God and continue the church, or live in a house that did not hinder my movement—and stop the church.

Right away, I told Papa Ron what God had said. "I am so thankful for your offer, but I will remain here until the church moves to our property. God has told me the church will not continue if I move from this house now. I don't want to value myself or my comfort more than the work of God."

Papa Ron replied, "I will send the money I promised, and you can do what you want with it. The decision is up to you. The money will be your personal funds."

And so, each month when the money came, I put the amount in a safe place, no matter how demanding thing got financially. I thought that Allen and I might need to use the funds for our rent at some time in the future.

We felt so blessed to own the land for our church, and our little congregation wanted to do something in the community to give back and to introduce ourselves. The heavily Islamic area was known for such bad things, it was time for something good. And so we decided to host a feeding program for the neighborhood children so they would be able to depend upon nutritious meals on a regular basis. As our church body of about thirty people were very poor, this decision was a great sacrifice. But we saw the feeding program as a way to show our neighbors God's love and care.

And God did exactly that. Over the years, the children come each month for a hot meal and activities like Bible stories and choir. We love these kids with everything we have.

▲▼▲

Allen and I decided to marry in my home district of Uganda. Many of my family believed I would never marry— and that it was not possible for me to have children. So much of my family and many friends lived there, and we wanted our union to be a great witness of what God can do.

We sent invitations to everyone to come on September 16th, 2006 to Kampala, Uganda. Newspapers and radio stations spread the word. Over 500 people came that day for a great time of commitment and celebration, and sharing the gospel. God has all the power.

What joy Allen and I experienced that day. My smile felt as wide as the whole country, as I held the hand of my new wife, and looked out at the faces of so many people who I loved, and who loved me.

Family who had lived through some of my darkest days. Brothers and sisters from churches, ministry, school days, and Bible college. Missionaries and friends from the United States. I felt wrapped up in the goodness of God and excited to continue in ministry with a wonderful, beautiful partner, so full of great potential.

After the wedding, Allen said, "You know, God spoke to me even before I met you that you were my husband., when you were on the steps at Pastor Isaac's church. I prayed for God to speak to you so that you would talk to me."

What joy it was to serve God with my beloved Allen. She truly became all that her mother said—becoming my legs, reaching and doing ministry alongside me.

Just a few months after our wedding, in December of 2006, two joyful things happened. The first was that Allen gave me the news that we were expecting a baby!

Praise to God flowed from my lips. As far back as I could remember, I had always loved children and longed for babies of my own. Many times, I had given up on the idea, thinking that it was impossible. And here, fatherhood was really going to happen. What an incredible gift from God.

The second joyful thing that month was the moment when we paid cash for our land. We had been praying for this possibility for more than a year, and with the help of World Outreach Ministries Foundation and those who donated, it came to pass. What a miracle-working God we serve—one who listens and answers the prayers of his people. Though this mission in Rwanda had seen huge obstacles, God had provided in every situation—even though sometimes it seemed at the last minute. Purchasing the land was such an encouragement to our church, and increased our faith. Faith we would rely on in the months ahead.

Shelter

MARCH OF 2007 arrived with several things to overcome. Many times, we long for God to only provide. We sometimes do not expect that we also have a part in that provision.

Allen was experiencing a complicated pregnancy, which made life hard for her. But despite all this, God had plans for Allen—plans she did not expect.

As a leader, I had learned through ministry in churches, schools, and Bible college that I needed to be aware of and identify gifts in people. When you spend time with your brothers and sisters, you notice things about them. However, all of us enjoy remaining in our comfort zone. I certainly felt this way when God told me to leave Uganda for Rwanda.

So I learned that if God could ask me to stretch myself, as a leader, I must do the same for my congregation. And Allen was a part of my congregation.

Allen was a talented and dedicated worship leader and had a call of God. She was gifted, especially in the area of prayer. When she prayed, you felt, "Wow!" When she worshiped, you felt, "Wow!" And when she taught, I felt the same thing.

God showed me even more potential hidden in her. Though she had not enjoyed a great education, she was bold and well-spoken.

"Why don't you think about preaching?" I asked her.

"Oh, I don't think so," she said. "I have only taught in a small group. Not to the whole church."

"Allen," I said. "God is telling you to raise up. If he sees the potential in you, he will give you what you need."

And so she began. Our church provided training for her. God spoke through Allen in such a powerful way. Her messages encouraged and challenged all of us. And then she even began getting invitations to preach in different churches. She preaches all over, even on the radio.

As for the church, we now owned our land, but we did not have money to construct a building. Meeting in the living room was illegal in Rwanda, but meeting in a temporary shelter was also illegal.

I took the matter to God. "How can we construct a church without money?"

God's message was clear. He spoke to my heart. *I have done my part. The remaining part is yours. Take a step of faith and go.*

It seemed that God wanted me to take that sum of money that Papa Ron had been sending towards a better house, and use it to build our church. The amount came to 450,000 Rwandan francs, a little less than $600 US at that time. That was all right with me, but what would my new bride think if I used those funds that way? I approached Allen and we prayed about what we should do.

Without pause, Allen said, "Honey, if God says yes, who am I to say no? Go and use it." This was yet another confirmation that I had been given a godly woman—the best wife I needed.

And so we took a step of faith, surrendering our only savings to build the house of God, emptying that account to give to the Lord. We believed God would take our small sacrifice and accomplish great things.

That Wednesday, we addressed our dear church family assembled in the increasingly cramped living room.

"God has asked us to step out in faith. This Sunday, we will hold the service on our church property."

Everyone expressed excitement and added to the fund. Most of our members did not have much income. They could have been selfish with their meager funds, but they knew God wanted to accomplish something important. Their response was such a great example of sacrificial giving.

On Thursday, we took the money we had collected and purchased enough tarps and poles to make a tent.

That Sunday we had such a great celebration on the property God had given us. We sang and danced and prayed, and God's word was heard in our little tent.

But our Muslim neighbors looked for an opportunity to shut us down. They had opposed our purchase of the property, not to mention the fact that I was a new person in the community, and had not yet earned their trust. They went to the authorities and complained.

Before long, the police came by. "Pastor, you must demolish this tent. You may only meet in a permanent structure. Your neighbors are complaining. Why don't you rent a building?"

But we had no money left. We stood on the dirt ground during services, as we had no chairs.

I did not take issue with their complaints. After all, it was true that we were not operating legally. I did not want to fight with them or accuse them. God would defend us. But God had told us to move forward, and so we did. And still, the church grew.

Soon after, two miracles happened.

In May, Lovie and Syvelle Phillips came with some missionary friends to visit and encourage us. They joined us in the temporary shelter for our worship service. The missionaries who came with Lovie and Syvelle offered to buy plastic chairs for the congregation that now numbered 150. What a blessing this was.

Another missionary in the same group offered us $2500 with which to build a better shelter and pay for the construction permit for the eventual church building.

With excitement, we spoke to the authorities, and it seemed that the construction permit would be approved. We purchased building materials: metal pillars, cement, and iron sheets for the roof.

However, when the officials came to our site and saw our materials standing ready, they refused to give us the permit.

"Why?" we asked.

Under Kigali's master plan, the officials wanted all buildings to match in structure, and they felt our church would not match with the city plan. With breaking hearts, we were forced to sell the things we had purchased.

However, God has his ways. We had already scheduled a large conference in July. Unsure of our reception, we went to ask for permission from the officials to hold the conference on the site. Soon after, we received a letter—with God's provision. The officials not only granted our request to hold the conference, but they also gave permission to improve the place. This gave us a great opportunity to enlarge our temporary shelter and make it more beautiful.

We purchased better tarps, and fixed everything in a very good way, doubling the size. The building's roof looked like the roof on a house and seemed fancy to us.

Challenges

AUGUST 8TH, 2007 turned out to be the greatest day for me. That day, my son came into the world.

When the labor came on, Allen and I went straight to the hospital. After we arrived, the doctors examined Allen and quickly determined that something was wrong. I prayed mightily that this miracle child would stay safe through his birth.

Finally, after many hours, the doctors decided that a cesarean section was necessary. The baby was in a complicated breech position, and the doctors could not cause the baby to move. Poor Allen was in terrible pain. The moments stretched as I waited for the doctor's report. At long last, the doctor came to tell me the news.

"You have a healthy son," he said. "It was good that he was born through surgery, for the umbilical cord was wrapped tightly around his neck and he might not have survived a normal birth."

Allen and I thanked God for his provision. We named our son Favor, for God had shown us much favor in giving us a child.

I wanted to shout to the world, "I have a son!" So many people thought a child was not possible for me, or expected a child of mine to be disabled. But little Favor was healthy in every way—and looked exactly like me. There was no doubt about his father.

▲▼▲

Our church continued meeting in the temporary shelter during this time, and God kept on blessing us with growth. However, that December, Favor developed a hernia at the age of four months. We prayed fervently for him, as his condition gave him much discomfort. It hurt me to see my son crying and reminded me how God feels about each one of the people he created when they experience pain. God felt the pain of my injuries and illnesses, just like he felt the the intense suffering of each person who suffered during and after the genocide.

In March of 2008, we discovered good news and bad news. Allen and I took Favor to the doctor to determine what could be done for his condition. But the doctors could find no evidence of a hernia! God had performed a miracle for Favor.

And Allen told me that we would be adding another child to the family at the end of the year.

At this same time, due to continued neighborhood complaints, the government in Kigali put an end to our use of the temporary shelter for church services.

We cried and we prayed, but we were determined. "We will continue to meet on our property," I said to the church body. "We are saving money toward building our first structure, and this is something we can do."

And so after one year in the temporary shelter, we began to meet in the open air. Sometimes the sun shone. Sometimes the skies poured down rain. Some who could afford them brought umbrellas, but ours was not a wealthy congregation. Those with umbrellas wanted to hold one over me as I preached.

"No," I said. "I must identify with all our members. I cannot preach in comfort while others get wet."

We met outside for three months and two weeks, and in May began to construct a small, permanent building. Again, we purchased building materials like metal, cement, stones, sand, and iron sheets, trying to make several purchases from some of the very neighbors who had tried to force us out through their complaints to the authorities.

Our first worship service in the shell of the new church was on June 26, 2008, conducted with great joy, even though construction was not complete. We had no windows or doors or floor, but that did not matter to us. We rejoiced that our challenge with the building was coming to an end. When we held our annual conference in the last week of July, we found the building could fit 300 people.

In early December that year, our son Precious joined our family. What fun and joy he brought to our lives! We so enjoyed his early months, alongside his big brother Favor, who was toddling around by this time.

▲▼▲

God directed me to begin a radio ministry. We now lived in a house that was more conducive for using my wheelchair, but I still found obstacles in many places I had to go. One of these was the studio where I did live radio broadcasts every week.

The building was one of the newest in the city but had no elevator. The studio sat on the sixth floor.

And so, each week when I went to the studio, I brought along my rubber boots and climbed the stairs to the studio. But just as God had told me so many years before as a teenager, my obedience was far more important than my mobility. And he blessed that radio ministry in many ways.

The main focus of the broadcast was to rebuild and restore foundations in our communities, churches, education—everywhere. One part of the radio broadcast were testimonies of people; those who were encouraged, those who asked Christ into their lives for the first time, and those who experienced healing or restoration. We heard so many amazing testimonies each week of what God was doing through the radio ministry.

One day, after giving my message, I was about to pray before signing off. God directed me to do something different.

"I am going to pray for you," I said into the microphone. "I feel that there is someone who is in need of healing from God. He has the power to do this. Lay your hand on the radio, and I will pray for you now."

The next day, I received a call from a woman in a village outside of Kigali. "I wish I could see you and that would be enough. God is amazing!" she said.

She told me that her brother had been paralyzed for two years. When she heard the radio show, she brought her brother near to put his hand on the radio. When that prayer ended, he stood up and walked!

She added, "You must be someone so special. That is why God is using you in such a mighty way."

I had to tell her the truth. "Even if God is using me, it is not because I am so special, but God is the great one. You do not know this, but I live with a physical disability like your brother, and cannot walk. Our God is no respecter of persons. He is able to do exceedingly beyond what we can imagine."

"What?" she exclaimed. "You cannot walk, and yet God heals others through you? God is a powerful God."

Miracles

IN APRIL OF 2009, I held a gospel crusade in an eastern province of Rwanda, about three hours from home. Some people brought a woman who was both blind and paralyzed. We prayed for her, and she received healing. She walked to our crusade the next day to testify of God's power.

At that crusade, God gave me a prophetic word about another woman who was there. I said, "God has told me that you should not leave your husband."

When the crusade was done, the woman came running to me, crying. She had packed all her things and had planned to divorce her husband, hiding her belongings with the neighbors. She received Jesus in her life that evening and chose to go back to her husband. We serve a miracle-working God.

But even as we continued to enjoy what God was doing in that crusade, the devil was busy plotting to destroy what was dear to me. I received a call at midnight that shook me deeply.

One of our good friends had delivered a baby. Allen took four-month-old Precious with her to pay a visit at the hospital. After leaving the hospital, Allen had been walking on the sidewalk, holding Precious on her hip, when a motorcycle lost control and hit them with incredible force.

The scene was chaotic, I learned. All the clothes Allen wore and the things she carried were reduced to rags. She lost hold of Precious when the motorcycle struck, and the baby was thrown to the tarmac road. Allen was injured, but Precious was completely fine. What a blessing!

My dear, sweet Allen and Precious. I longed to be with them right away, but I had to wait until morning for someone to drive me the three hours back home. I prayed for them with such intensity all night long.

But the news at the hospital was grave. Allen suffered a leg broken in two places, but most concerning was her head injury. A skull fracture and bleeding on her brain left her in a coma, and the doctors had no idea if she would recover or not. Allen's beautiful face was so swollen, she was almost unrecognizable. Even 20-month-old Favor cried in fear when he saw his mama. Catrine came to care for Favor and Precious, as I spent time at Allen's side, praying continually.

Days passed by with no change in her condition. The devil tried to attack my mind during this time, saying, "If you really serve God, why can't he protect your family?"

I had to stay on my guard and refute those wrong voices. I knew that God was faithful in every circumstance—even this. Serving God does not mean that the devil will never attack our lives or our family. But one thing I am so sure of is that he will give us strength and turn what the enemy meant for evil into good.

I made a choice to praise God despite Allen's critical condition. Was it not yesterday that God had healed the blind and paralyzed woman? I believed God would intervene in Allen's life with his healing hand.

Sometimes I heard other people whispering, "So sad. They will both be in wheelchairs, and who will heal them?" Others believed Allen would die. Though it was difficult, I kept my faith, even during her coma. I knew that God would work out something special.

After two long weeks, and endless prayers, Allen opened her eyes.

I gripped her hands and smiled into her dear face. "Oh, my beautiful Allen, it is so good to see you. And so much has happened while you slept."

During her third week in the hospital, Allen experienced rapid healing of her skull and underwent surgery for her leg. A few days later, she was ready for discharge.

I felt a burden to go through the ward and pray for the sick people who were in critical condition, as Allen had been.

One lady from Burundi had been in that hospital for two years. She had experienced bleeding since the first day of her marriage. After prayer, God healed her instantly. She was so happy to see God do this for her.

Another person had been in some kind of accident, like Allen. On the left side of the man's body, x-rays had revealed that everything was broken—his leg, his arm, even his hand—all in multiple places. His limbs were swathed in thick bandages, and he writhed in pain. I laid hands on him and prayed for his healing. He was scheduled for surgery in a few days.

Allen finally came home but had to use crutches for two months. What a pair we made, but how thankful we were! We believed God for complete healing and continued to work hard to see the church building fully done.

Allen holding Favor not long after the accident. The scar from her head injury is visible. I am holding Precious, who was unharmed.

Two days later, I received a phone call from the man I had prayed for in the hospital.

"Pastor, God healed my arm and my leg!"

My eyebrows raised. "What happened? Did you have surgery?"

"When I went for the second x-ray before surgery, they found that the bones in my leg and my arm were knit together—as if they had never been broken. The doctors were so surprised. God healed me!"

I rejoiced with him and praised God. His ways are not our ways.

Then the man added, "But could you pray for my hand? That is the only thing still broken."

I shared with him my own story of God's wisdom of when he heals and when he waits. "If we trust God with all our hearts, God has unlimited power to heal and deliver those who need his intervention. Our God is not limited to work by what you are going through or the pain you might be experiencing today. Do not lower God to the standard of your problems. His power is unlimited to all who trust in him."

And then I prayed to ask God to join the bones of his hand together.

For so long I thought I was limited because God did not say yes to my prayers for healing immediately. But God said yes to my desire to be useful. And he knew that I would be more useful to him if he said no to my healing. I determined I would obey his voice, even in my wheelchair.

I know my God. He has power to heal, to deliver, to set someone free. God has healed my inner man, even if he doesn't heal my body. It is up to God to do what he is willing to do. And so it is for you. I am a man who believes that God can heal me anytime, but my waiting for my healing will never distract me from fulfilling my heavenly assignment. I do not judge myself because of my physical disability. For this reason, it doesn't stop me from praying for others to receive their miracles and healings.

Light

TOWARDS THE END of November, our church building was finally finished and furnished. We planned to have a great celebration on December 6th to coincide with the 4-year anniversary of the start of Nyabugingo Worship Center. And that fall, we found that we were expecting our third child.

That December day was wonderful. We invited so many friends to celebrate the new building and the continued ministry of our church. God had done a great victory. The entire community showed up. Pastors came, including Pastor Steve Mayanja. Government officials attended, even members of parliament. Different people testified—some of whom had been against our church from the start.

Even as we celebrated four years of the church, and the official opening of the church building, in my heart I was also celebrating that God had preserved the life of my dear wife and ministry partner, and our beloved son, Precious.

What a great victory. God can change what we thought was the worst of our time, to make it the best of our time.

Many friends came to celebrate the new building.

Today, Nyabugingo Worship Center is joined by a second church we planted. We actively minister to everyone who comes our way, including individuals who were harmed by genocide, or who perpetrated the genocide. God has been so good to minister to people in a way that has helped them to extend radical forgiveness.

Forgiveness is not easy. Many times a person will approach one of our church members and say, "I killed your family in the genocide. Will you forgive me?"

Someone told me once that God could not forgive what happened in Rwanda. But Jesus said we must love our neighbor; love our enemies and bless those who curse us. And I found many people who have forgiven far more than I had to forgive in my life. One man had scars all over his body and his head. He forgave those who cut him with the machete. I have no scars. If he could forgive those who harmed him, what about me?

The survivors of the genocide have taught me many great lessons in forgiveness. Some are now disabled from their injuries in 1994. They still suffer in pain, yet they forgive and set their enemies free. Why not me? As a new believer, I had started to forgive, but the genocide accelerated the process. I released the bitterness in my heart. There is not anything we can't forgive, for Jesus went to the cross and sacrificed everything for us.

But we must realize forgiveness is gradual—it keeps on coming, and so it is not instant. We expect forgiveness to come from heaven, but we must choose it. Many people remain in that place of pain and bitterness. Our church longs to walk alongside them, comfort them, and offer them hope through Jesus.

In our church, we have both members who suffered much during the genocide, and members who participated in the killings. Now these dear people sit and fellowship together as one body, unified and reconciled in Jesus. God is so good.

▲▼▲

What the nation of Rwanda went through is hard to explain. The sense of isolation when tragedy struck made us wonder where the world was when all this happened. Rwanda is small—similar in size to the US state of New Jersey. The country did not have massive economic and natural resources to attract the interest of developers. And so we felt as if Rwanda died—but God resurrected our beloved country.

There was a time when people were ashamed to be called Rwandan, even in other countries. Some Rwandans changed their names in order to fit in to the societies in which they lived. Glory be to God that those days are over!

We no longer have identification cards that say Hutu or Tutsi or Twa, because we are all Rwandese. I am so proud of where we are as a nation and our home-grown solutions are working. Our government has put intense effort into seeing that our country is well-governed and that corruption is not tolerated, and makes sure that the rule of law is practiced in a society which once was wild. The country with such a tragic history is now one of the safest, and most conducive for economic development, with some of the happiest people you can find.

Each month, the entire nation, from the president on down, participates in Umugandu Day. This is a day of community service to beautify our country, and a chance to gather in 'town meetings' to work out differences.

The church in Rwanda is stronger than ever. I want to thank God for the church, which has ministered healing to the hearts of people that felt beyond repair. The word of God we and others preach has tremendously changed our nation. We bless God for all the missionaries and volunteers who came and gave of themselves during this time when darkness hovered over a land of a thousand hills.

Praise God for his light that dispels the darkness.

Unlimited

WHAT DOES IT mean to conquer on your knees? My brothers and sisters, start with prayer, since prayer in faith moves mountains.

My biggest mountain—my disability—was too big for me to move on my own. Though I had many inabilities, through prayer and intercession something new was birthed in my life. I tried to suppress it, but I could not. The more intimacy I found with God through prayer, the more my hope rose up. I felt it in my heart, but I could not touch it in the physical arena. My way of living, appearance, and environment dictated everything. Most people could not see a future for me. Something untangled and resonated in my heart. Though I tried, it could not be silenced. Though my situation tried to press it down, it could not be subdued. I doubted, but inside my heart it was a dream that could become reality. I cried and worried a great deal, but this idea of becoming someone kept on returning.

I constantly felt that empty vacuum that could not be filled by anything else. I had so many questions, but I had no one to give me the true answers I needed.

Insecurities flooded through me; many fears of what would come next. Today I realize that those were the labor pains of destiny; this was when the child was about to be born. There must be qualified personnel to guide me in the process and I even needed the power to push so that this baby called destiny would be embraced. Instead of pushing this baby called destiny, I just wanted to murder or kidnap him. This is why I wanted to commit suicide, because my destiny was not realized in my earlier days. When destiny is not realized, you are always limited. But when destiny is discovered, you are always unlimited.

After many days of denying this fact, I decided to take God at his word if I was to become a true follower of Jesus. I love this scripture in John 14:15. Jesus said, "If you love me, you will keep my commandments." I loved Jesus with all my heart, but I felt I needed a detailed plan for my life. I hated to stay in the past, but the past still seemed to dictate to me. I wouldn't allow the past to hold my future. In all my prayers, I always looked for an exit door. Though I was not sure how, I became convinced that one day I would be out of this life of misery. I would be useful and of help to others someday.

I have been fully convinced that when I am on my knees praying, that is where I draw and fetch my power and strength to do the impossible. A true prayer life mobilizes and awakens hidden potential in us. Prayer is where hidden treasures are excavated. Prayer is where undisclosed mines of wealth and resources are tapped. With prayer, the stock of hidden talents God deposited in us is opened up for proper use. You are unlimited whenever you allow what is in you to come out.

On your knees, is where the great research of self-discovery is done. This is where the purpose of life and sense of living is downloaded. In prayer, is where your identity and future destiny are defined. For me, this journey has not been easy, but at times it has been enjoyable, more so while going against the odds. When you break the cocoon you have been confined in, this is when your life is truly defined. You're too rich to die in that miserable life. There are so many people waiting to tap what God has deposited in you.

Don't let your life end before you fully maximize the potential and treasures hidden in you. You have much more to offer to this world than you have ever imagined. Nothing can limit what God has deposited in you. What is in you is unlimited. No power, no authority, nor any wall can stop what God has started in your life.

Any call or vision from God always begins as a mountain of impossibilities, but each task is always accomplished systematically in faith and in obedience. There are new unlocked doors you need to venture into whenever you stop limiting yourself.

You and I have a big debt to pay. God demands us to put to use all the resources he has deposited in us before we die. Through spending time in his presence, the best comes out of us. I like what D.L. Moody said, "He who kneels the most, stands the best."

The power of God's kingdom is manifested on earth whenever we pray, and prayer gives a master key to the children of God—which makes them unlimited.

Today you can say yes to God and pray this prayer with me.

Dear God in heaven,

I come to you in the name of Jesus. I acknowledge to You that I have done wrong, and I am sorry for those things and the life that I have lived; I need your forgiveness.

I believe that your only begotten Son Jesus Christ shed His precious blood on the cross at Calvary and died for the wrongs I have done, and I am now willing to turn from those things.

You said in Your Holy Word, Romans 10:9 that if we confess the Lord our God and believe in our hearts that God raised Jesus from the dead, we shall be saved.

Right now I confess Jesus as the Lord of my soul. With my heart, I believe that God raised Jesus from the dead. This very moment I accept Jesus Christ as my own personal Savior and according to His Word, right now I am saved.

Thank you, Jesus for your unlimited grace which has saved me from the wrong I have done. I thank you Jesus that your grace never leads to license, but rather it always leads to repentance. Therefore, Lord Jesus transform my life so that I may bring glory and honor to you alone and not to myself.

Thank you Jesus for dying for me and giving me eternal life.

AMEN.

May God bless you as you become unlimited.

Canisius Gacura serves as senior pastor of Nyabugingo Worship Center and president of Rwanda Christian Outreach Ministries. He has a Bachelor of Theology degree from Yesu Akwagala Bible College, affiliated with Seattle Bible College.

He is married to his beautiful wife, Allen, and is the father of three sons and one daughter, named Favour, Precious, Purity, and Prize. He began serving God at the age of fifteen and entered full-time ministry in 2005.

Pastor Gacura conducts conferences, church planting, world missions, evangelistic crusades, leadership trainings, and pastors' conferences. He is a preacher/teacher, a mentor, a coach, and an international motivational speaker.

Canisius Gacura

Acknowledgements

I WOULD LIKE TO thank my wife Allen and our four children, Favour, Precious, Purity and Prize. Your dedication, encouragement, support, prayers, advice, and love have made my life—and this project a success.

Pastor Syvelle and Lovie Phillips: You have been my heroes and I am what I am because you allowed God to become a channel of blessing in my life. From the bottom of my heart, I would like to appreciate you for being there for me and believing in me when no one could have done it. Your support, both financial and spiritual, has made a big mark on my life.

Pastor Ron and Shirley DeVore: Your heart to reach the lost whatever the cost has been so contagious and I thank you for all your good examples of being true missionaries. Your love for people, for missions, and for God's work has been magnetic. Your spiritual and financial support has blessed me, and you have been a true mother and father to me.

Debbie Maxwell Allen: I would like to acknowledge you for the great work you have done. You have made this dream, which I had for years, become a reality. It is going to be in the record, that a vision God gave me for years became true through you. Thank you for the great impact you have made on my life. May God richly bless you for all the sleepless nights you invested in this book.

Dr. Dan Hammer: You have been a great partner to our mission, and we are so proud that you are one of the spiritual fathers of our mission. Your life speaks louder than your words.

Dr. Steven Damulira Mayanja: You have been a true spiritual father and a great encouragement to my life. I greatly appreciate you.

Pastor David Pepper: There are many ways you have greatly impacted my life, but I will mention two. Your first invitation to the States launched me into a new dimension of ministry and fulfilled what God had spoken for several years. Additionally, your invitation to be a storyteller in your missions book, *Declare It Fearlessly*, made this new life-changing project a possibility.

All my pastors: My dear pastors, during the time I was in your hands, your touch, your prayers, your messages, faith, and visions, grounded me on the foundation. You helped me discover my destiny. My words are limited, and I don't know how to say thank you for the big difference you made to the guy who was in a deep pit. I celebrate in victory for the wonderful work you have done. God has used you beyond what words can mention.

All my teachers: Thank you for your impartation, your encouragements, passing on your knowledge and experience, bearing all my challenges, and the love of God you showered upon my life, causing me to soar into my destiny. Your selfless sacrifices mean more than you can think.

My WOMF co-workers: What a wonderful group to belong to! I am so blessed to be one of you. Your affirmation of my call, your encouragement, love, example in life, visits, prayers, mission-oriented attitudes, have positioned me where I am today. Thank you. I would like to especially thank Pastor Steve Kaweesa. The first visit to mark my promised land in Rwanda was through you. Thank you for that ride, which opened a great door of what we are seeing God doing in this great nation of Rwanda.

All missionaries and ministry partners worldwide: You have no idea how much you have accomplished in the kingdom of God through your sponsorships, encouragement, prayers, gifts, mission trips, teachings, preachings, and investment in projects. Your faith in action has made impossibilities possibilities.

Pastor Ed Pohlreich: Your invitation to attend Bible college and your determination to carry me even on your back in case I could not crawl to classes, paved a way for a new dimension of my life.

Pastor Scott and Brenda Volz: My first touch of the computer was through your exposure. You opened my eyes to a new world of technology. Thank you for being a part of what God is doing in my life. Your contribution has made a big difference.

Pastor Dave Easterly: Your message about vision acted as a great catalyst of what God was doing in my life. You helped me to define my destiny. Your support for my first visit to Rwanda and your constant visits meant the whole world to me. A big thank you to you, my friend.

Rwanda Christian Outreach Ministries Board of Directors: My sincere thanks to my co-workers in Rwanda's field. Your wisdom, prayers, and spiritual support has made God's vineyard in Rwanda flourish. I want to especially mention Mr. James Karimba. You and your family embraced me like a family member, which caused me to fly like an eagle on my journey of calling. I'm so thankful for you. Pastor Isaac: you and your wife Jane have been a great pillar in the transformation of my life, and my response to the call of God. I'm so proud of you, and you are true shepherds. May God continue to pour his power and blessings upon your life.

Nyabugingo Worship Centre members: My flock, you mean the whole world to me. I'm so proud to be your pastor. Your lives always act as an anchor, which keeps me moving each and every day. I love you and treasure you more than you can think. I look forward to what the future holds for us. May God continue to enlarge your territories in all moments of your life. Through you the kingdom of God will be reflected to all people around the nations. Let our light continue to shine for his glory.

My dear parents, Francis Kinyogote and Mukandekezi: Through you, I came into the world. I could not be what I am today without you. You will always be my parents. I greatly honor and treasure you.

Friends: For my life to be what it is, an endless list of people have been instrumental in shaping my life. Each one of your contributions made a tremendous impact on every achievement of my life. Pushing my wheelchair, bringing me food or water, riding me on bicycles, motorcycles, or in cars, prayers, encouragements, and love. You affected my life in an unimaginable way.

Were I to mention each person of impact on my life, the list would be endless. Thank you to each of you, but most of all to my God and Savior, Jesus Christ.

Debbie Maxwell Allen works as a project manager for Good Catch Publishing and as a freelance editor. She graduated from Columbia International University with a Bachelors Degree in Elementary Education. In her spare time, she writes young adult novels in the Rocky Mountains, alongside her husband, two cats, one dog, and whichever of her five children are home at the moment.

Debbie Maxwell Allen
Acknowledgements

THE FIRST TIME I spoke on the phone with a soft-spoken Rwandan pastor, I knew that his was a life-changing story. I am so grateful for the faithful example of Canisius Gacura's life, and how with God's help, he has turned trials into triumphs. It has been an honor to partner with him on this book. And I later discovered that this pastor is not as soft-spoken as I thought! If you ever have a chance to hear this man of God speak, make it a priority. You will not soon forget his words.

So many people came together to make this book a reality. I want to thank my editors, Shelly Worscheck and Katie Allen for finding the errors I could no longer see. Shelly went above and beyond, despite unexpected deadlines, and this book is better for it. To Lois Rosio Sprague, the cover painting is amazing. I wish you could have presented it to Pastor Gacura yourself. Scoti Domeij, you put in so many hours on the cover, pouring yourself into this project. I am so grateful.

Creative friends are a great blessing. I can count several who offered their expertise and much-needed advice. Jim Maxwell was instrumental in choosing the title. Shelley

Ring and Dawn McKenna and Marla Benroth for publishing tips. Katie Allen and Mike DeHerrera for marketing skills.

And then there are all those who came alongside and held my arms up when I felt weary. My husband Matt, long-suffering, and willing to put up with my crazy hours, while he ended up doing dishes, laundry, and cleaning the house. I love you. My children, Keith, Katie, Emily & Josh, Daniel, and Jonathan—for your encouragement and belief. My sister Lisa, always ready to listen and pray and help in sacrificial ways. My parents, Jim and Nancy Maxwell and Bim and Tuni Allen, for faithfully praying this project through.

I also want to thank Lois, Lorrie, and Laura, my prayer group, for sticking with me for so many years, and keeping me going. And for my QMT writing group, Shelly, Angela, and Kelley, for holding my feet to the fire with my goals, and just understanding what the journey is like.

Thanks also to Gary and Lois Sprague, innkeepers at the beautiful Lodge at Elk Valley in Divide, Colorado, for generously offering a location for this book's beginning and end. And Kelly Tucker for above-and-beyond hospitality.

Much appreciation goes to Woodland Park Community Church and Nyabugingo Worship Centre for your faithful prayers. I have not yet met my Rwandan brothers and sisters, but your prayers were felt halfway around the world.

Any beauty in this book belongs to the story—truth, no matter how raw, possesses a beauty that draws us in and brings change. May you be changed, as I have.

Vision

AND YOUR ANCIENT RUINS shall be rebuilt; you shall raise up the foundations of buildings that have laid waste for many generations; and you shall be called Repairer of the Breach, Restorer of Streets to Dwell In. ~Isaiah 58:12

RWANDA CHRISTRIAN

OUTREACH MINISTRIES

Ministry Vision

Our hearts desire is to restore the foundations and to reach nations with the unchanging gospel of our Lord Jesus Christ at whatever the cost.

Thank you for partnering with us through your purchase of this book! Our vision is for foundations to be restored in families, in communities, in education, in government, in churches—in every area. Rwanda Christian Outreach Ministries is based upon God's will.

Whatever door is opened to us, we will walk through, if it is God's will.

Unlimited

Would you join us in continuing to reach out to the healing country of Rwanda and beyond? All donations are tax-deductible. Find out more at World Outreach Ministry Foundation. http://womf.org/

Planting of churches:
Establish ministry centres
Promote unity in the body of Christ
Intercede for Rwanda and her leadership
Encourage 40 days of national prayer & fasting for revival
Education institutions:
Primary schools
Secondary schools
Vocational schools
Bible colleges, Universities
Community Centres
Evangelism:
Monthly crusades
Distribute aids for the crippled, blind, and deaf
Prison outreaches
Hospital outreaches
Door to door evangelism
School outreaches
Films based on the word of God
Radio ministry
Conferences:
General conference
Women's conferences
Youth conferences
Pastors and leadership conferences
Children's conferences
Prayer conferences
Leadership trainings
Revival conferences

Charity:
Orphanage homes
Homes for the disabled
Programs to help needy children and communities
access quality education
Assist the poor, widows, and single parents by
teaching entrepreneurship
Help rural pastors in ministry
Establish hospitals and health dispensaries

Our planned new building under construction.

Connect

THANK YOU SO MUCH for taking the time to read *Unlimited*. I would be so grateful if you took a moment to add a review to the book page on Amazon. Reviews are wonderful for authors—and they only need to be a few sentences. If you would like to stay connected, see below.

Unlimited Website: http://unlimitedbook.org/
- Find pictures, Pastor Gacura's blog, and small group discussion questions
- Join our newsletter and get **free downloadable signed bookplates**

Facebook: https://www.facebook.com/ UnlimitedConqueringOnMyKnees

Pinterest: http://bit.ly/unlimited-pinterest

Twitter: https://twitter.com/gacuracanisius

Church website: Rwanda Christian Outreach Ministries: http://rwacom.org/

World Outreach Ministries Foundation: http://womf.org/

To contact Pastor Gacura for speaking engagements, use one of the following:
unlimited.conqueringonmyknees@gmail.com
kanisiousk@yahoo.com
gacuraallenrwacom@gmail.com

Conquering on My Knees

Afterwords

I AM PROUD TO claim Canisius Gacura as my African son. My own son, Phil Phillips, and Canisius consider each other as brothers. We love and admire him. When Canisius came to our children's home and school in Uganda, he pulled himself with his hands, as he had no use of his legs. He had to wear six mismatched shoes in order to maneuver around. The first time I saw him, he crawled towards me dragging the boots he wore on his knees, shoes on his feet, and wearing flip-flops on his hands. What amazed me was that he never looked dirty. I was so grateful that we were able to bless him with his first wheelchair.

Even though he was fifteen, he had to start school as a second grader. Canisius excelled and continued to do so all the way through high school. We were so proud of him. He shared with us his desire to attend Bible college. My husband Syvelle and I began searching for a Bible college. Sadly, most of Africa automatically considers those who are handicapped as being worthless. Several theological seminaries would not even consider him.

My husband was the speaker almost annually at the pastors' conference in Seguku, Uganda. We were ecstatic with the announcement that they were starting a Bible college during the fall season. The previous Dean of Students said Canisius couldn't attend because he was handicapped. However, I must admit I was excited when I learned that one of my missionary friends was going to take the place of the former Dean of Students. When I called, his response was, "Of course, you can send him. Even if I have to carry him on my back, he must come." Well, he never had to carry him on his back. Dr. Hammer made it clear that Canisius handled those hills very well without any help.

Today, Pastor Canisius is a great preacher of the gospel around the world. He also pastors a good, strong church that he planted in Rwanda and is married to a beautiful, godly wife with four lovely children. While he is away, she takes the responsibility of the church and also preaches to the congregation. I love his family more than I have words to express. I know this book will inspire you tremendously the way Canisius Gacura's life has inspired me.

Lovie E. Phillips

Founder, God Loves Kids http://godloveskids.com/

My family with Lovie Phillips and her son, Phil Phillips.

Pastor Canisius Gacura has written a must-read book, titled *Unlimited*. For those struggling with inferiority complexes, those who don't think they have what it takes to serve God, or to be a missionary, pastor, those with emotional disabilities, physical disabilities, fears of any kind, those who want to go in ministry, and most of all, those of us who are called by God and given responsibilities to raise up leaders, fathers, mothers, guardians who raise up children and spiritual fathers and mothers who are called by God to train and prepare people for ministry.

When God called me to raise for him World
Changers, he spoke to me, "Don't look at their outside
appearance. Look beyond their outside appearance when I
bring them to you." (1 Samuel 16:7) God told me, "When I
called David, he started building his army with all those who
were in distress, depressed or discontented, those the world
had rejected. He become their leader, he trained them and
they became Great Warriors of their season and for David's
kingdom." (1Samuel 22:2) "So, as you train and prepare for
me the Spiritual army and World Changers, I will bring to
you even those of whom the world doesn't see potential,
those the world believes they don't deserve their time, energy
and resources, and you build me an army out of them!

When Gacura came to our mission, Uganda Christian
Outreach Ministries headquarters, to receive ministry training
at our Bible college, Yesu Akwagala Bible College (Jesus
Loves You Bible College), he also became a member of our
church, Seguku Worship Center. Those who see with natural
eyes did not recognize his potential and abilities, because you
needed to look through spiritual eyes by the Holy Spirit to
see the powerful man inside.

He showed his determination, zeal to serve God, and availability to serve others in his willingness to go door-to-door in our village, joining the church choir, being a member of our intercessors team, waking up in the nights to seek God, and climbing the hill from our church up to the Bible College. He refused anyone to carry him, feel sorry for him, or look at him as a disabled beggar. He knew who he was and whose he is—belonging to God. The anointing upon his life, the call upon his life, and the power of the Holy Spirit in him did not allow his physical disabilities to stand in his way or became his excuses.

I have seen Gacura running his race of faith through training at the Bible College, starting Rwanda Christian Outreach Ministries in Kigali Rwanda, launching the church, Nyabugingo Worship Center in an outcast area of Kigali City, where he serves as the senior pastor. He found his beautiful wife Allen, and today they have four beautiful children. He is a living testimony of what the Holy Spirit can do in any vessel yielded to God. He has surprised all those who thought he would never marry, or produce children, or flourish in any area of life.

As you read through his book, be ready to be challenged, motivated and inspired to go where you have never gone before, to do what you have never done before, and to achieve what you or others thought you would never achieve in your life.

Canisius Gacura is a pastor, leader, and motivational speaker. I highly recommend my spiritual son, my friend, and his book to you.

Dr. Pastor Steven D. Mayanja
Senior Pastor Seguku Worship Center, Kampala, Uganda
Founder Uganda Christian Outreach Ministries,
http://www.yesuakwagala.com/
Director of Africa Ministry Development (WOMF) World
Outreach Ministry Foundation

Some of my WOMF colleagues. Left to right: Shirley & Ron DeVore, Pastor Steve Mayanja, Shirley Mayanja, Elijah Mayanja

When Canisius Gacura arrived at our Yesu Akwagala Bible College to begin his first term, he had a well-used wheelchair as his mode of transportation. We looked at this small young man and his wheelchair, and at the great mountain that rose up behind the college. To our eyes, we saw the impossibilities of his daily routine. But with the eyes of faith and the God who can move mountains, Gacura accepted the challenge.

Without complaint and with a joyful heart, he conquered all the mountains set before him. He became an excellent student, a mentor to others, and an outstanding example of God's faithfulness to those willing to step out in faith to overcome their impossibilities and allow God to show us that in Him all things are possible. He completed his four years with high honors.

We were so proud to send him off to represent World Outreach Ministries in Rwanda. He once again was chosen to test his faith, but God has walked beside him and has shown himself strong on his behalf. Gacura and his wife Allen and four children have built a great ministry. They have mountain-moving faith to conquer the nation of Rwanda for God.

Gacura we are so proud to call you our son. We believe in you and know that with God, nothing is impossible.

Missionaries Ron and Shirley DeVore
President and Founder, World Outreach Ministry Foundation

In the journey of life there are a handful of people you encounter that define a word. You are about to meet one of those rare individuals in this book. A man that has overcome numerous obstacles, his narrative will inspire you to hope and believe that nothing is too difficult to face when the courageous love of Christ apprehends you. Perseverance in my dictionary is defined simply in two words . . . Canisius Gacura.

David Pepper
Founder, Amazon Outreach
http://amazon-outreach.org/

36302814R00227

Made in the USA
Middletown, DE
30 October 2016